Lecture Notes in Computer Science

Lecture Notes in Computer Science

Edited by G. Goos and J. Hartmanis

129

Brent T. Hailpern

Verifying
Concurrent Processes
Using Temporal Logic

Springer-Verlag
Berlin Heidelberg New York 1982

Editorial Board

W. Brauer P. Brinch Hansen D. Gries C. Moler G. Seegmüller
J. Stoer N. Wirth

Author

Brent T. Hailpern
IBM Thomas J. Watson Research Center
P.O.Box 218, Yorktown Heights, NY 10598, USA

CR Subject Classifications (1981): 5.21 5.24

ISBN 3-540-11205-7 Springer-Verlag Berlin Heidelberg New York
ISBN 0-387-11205-7 Springer-Verlag New York Heidelberg Berlin

This work is subject to copyright. All rights are reserved, whether the whole or part of the material
is concerned, specifically those of translation, reprinting, re-use of illustrations, broadcasting,
reproduction by photocopying machine or similar means, and storage in data banks. Under
§ 54 of the German Copyright Law where copies are made for other than private use, a fee is
payable to "Verwertungsgesellschaft Wort", Munich.
© by Springer-Verlag Berlin Heidelberg 1982
Printed in Germany

Printing and binding: Beltz Offsetdruck, Hemsbach/Bergstr.
2145/3140-543210

Acknowledgments

Years ago, my parents taught me to love learning. I thank them for that lesson and for their love; for without either one, this thesis would never have been written.

Many people at Stanford contributed in one way or another to this thesis. John Hennessy and Gio Wiederhold, as members of my reading committee, provided me with many useful comments and suggestions. John Gilbert, Jim Boyce, and Shel Finkelstein helped me understand the beauty of formal logic in general and temporal logic in particular. Robert Tarjan guided me through my first year at Stanford with his wisdom and his inexhaustable common sense. To these people and to the faculty, staff, and students of the Stanford Computer Science Department, I express my gratitude.

I want give special thanks to two of my dearest friends: David Wall and Richard Pattis. They provided constant professional and emotional support during my entire graduate career. The two of them were always there when I needed advice, someone to listen to me complain, a sounding board, criticism, or companionship. They contributed greatly to this thesis by reading various drafts and providing numerous comments.

There are no words to express my gratitude to Susan Owicki, my advisor. She introduced me to program verification and to temporal logic. Her ideas, comments, advice, and suggestions form an integral part of this thesis. It has been a great honor to have known her and to have worked with her.

I dedicate this thesis to my wife, Susan. Her love, support, and understanding gave me the strength to write this thesis. I am in her debt for the many hours I spent working when we could have been together, and I   look forward to spending the rest of my life discharging that debt.

My research was supported by a number of agencies, and I gratefully acknowledge their generosity. My graduate education was funded primarily by fellowships from the National Science Foundation and the Fannie and John Hertz Foundation. I received additional support from teaching assistantships in the Stanford Computer Science Department and Computer System Laboratory and from research assistantships with the S-1 project and my advisor. (The S-1 project is supported at Lawerence Livermore Laboratory of the University of California by the Department of the Navy via ONR Order No. N00014-78-F0023. Research with my advisor was supported by the Joint Services Electronics Project, under contract N-00014-75-C-0601. JSEP also funded my travel expenses in connection with this research.)

Abstract

Concurrent processes can exhibit extremely complicated behavior, and neither informal reasoning nor testing is reliable enough to establish their correctness. In this thesis, we develop a new technique for the verification of parallel programs. The technique is stated in terms of axioms and inference rules, and it is used to prove safety and liveness properties of parallel programs. Safety properties are assertions that must be satisfied by the system state at all times; they are analogous to partial correctness. Liveness properties refer to events that will occur in the future, such as program termination or the eventual receipt of a message. In addition to the formal proof rules, we present several heuristics to aid in the preparation of correctness proofs.

We model a parallel program as a set of interacting modules (processes and monitors), and we exploit this modularity in the verification process. First we prove properties of the low-level modules directly from their code. We then combine the specifications of the low-level modules to prove properties of higher-level modules, without again referring to the code. Eventually, we prove properties of the entire program.

We discuss the application of this verification technique to two classes of parallel programs: network protocols and resource allocators. Most previous approaches to verifying network protocols have been based upon reachability arguments for finite-state models of the protocols. Only protocols of limited complexity can be verified using the finite-state model, because of the combinatorial explosion of the state space as the complexity of the protocol increases. In contrast, our approach allows us to abstract information from the details of the implementation, so that the proof need not grow unmanageably as the protocol size increases.

The discussion of resource allocation centers around Hoare's structured paging system, which is a complex hierarchical program. With this example, we demonstrate that many of the techniques used in program verification can be used for specification as well.

The thesis also describes a number of tools that have been useful in proving concurrent programs. Two of the most important are history variables and temporal logic. We employ history variables to record the interaction between the modules that constitute a program. Temporal logic serves as a convenient notation for stating and proving liveness properties.

Table of Contents

Abstract

Acknowledgments

Table of Contents

List of Figures

List of Figures

Chapter 1
Introduction

In this thesis we present a technique for proving both safety and liveness properties of parallel programs. Safety properties are assertions that must be satisfied by the system state at all times; they are analogous to partial correctness. Liveness properties refer to events that will occur in the future, such as program termination or the eventual execution of an instruction. We describe new tools for verifying programs and heuristics for developing proofs. We demonstrate the applicability of the technique by proving the correctness of a number of algorithms from the literature in the areas of network protocols and resource allocation. The spirit of this thesis, however, is concerned with the design of programs.

Why should the main theme of a verification thesis be program design? The answer comes from the definition of verification. Verification is the science (art?) of showing that a program meets its specifications. The correctness proof of a program contains three parts: a program, its specifications, and a proof. In practice, showing that a program and a set of specifications correspond is extremely difficult. There are too many facts that can be deduced from each program statement, and there are too many ways in which these facts can be arranged. In addition, some program constructs, such as goto, only confuse matters due to their complicated inference rules. The day of the "automatic verifier"—when a program and its specifications are put in one end and the word *verified*, or the word *incorrect*, comes out the other—is not at hand and may never be. Practical verification requires building a program and its specifications at the same time, using one as a check against the other. The proof step only confirms that the building process is being conducted correctly.

The design methodology presented in this thesis, under the guise of verification, consists of four steps: organize the solution by breaking the problem into small subproblems with simple interfaces; write the code and the specifications for each subproblem; show that the solution for each subproblem matches its specification; and prove that the sum of the parts does what it is supposed to do. The first two steps are called *structured programming*, and they are well known to the computer science community. The third and fourth steps are verification. The main contribution of this thesis is to the third and fourth steps. Verification is not testing, it is not debugging, nor is it a last-minute pass to make sure that the program is correct. Verification should be a part of writing a program just like a syntax check of the code, or a run-time type-equivalence check of the assignment statements.

1. Introduction

Chapter 2 of this thesis describes our model of a concurrent program: a set of interacting processes and monitors. It is a short chapter, which introduces some important parallel program constructs and the programming language used in the rest of the thesis.

Chapter 3 supplies a historical perspective. The verification techniques in this thesis follow the tradition begun by Floyd. That tradition is detailed along with the ideas that form the cornerstones for my techniques.

Chapter 4 introduces the major new tool used in this thesis, temporal logic. Temporal logic is a convenient notation for describing liveness properties of programs. In this chapter, we describe the syntax, semantics, and history of temporal logic.

Chapter 5 describes how to verify parallel programs. The field still has the flavor of an art, and there are no hard-and-fast rules. Instead guidelines, helpful hints, and heuristics are presented to lead the uninitiated reader gently into the promised land of verification.

Chapter 6 contains the major new results of the thesis, the verification of network protocols using high-level language representations. Previous work in the field has been limited to proving safety properties of high-level descriptions (that is, if the protocol ever runs then it runs correctly), or liveness properties of finite-state representations of the protocols, but not both at the same time. Three examples are presented in this chapter: the alternating bit protocol, Stenning's data transfer protocol, and Brinch Hansen's multiprocessor network.

Chapter 7 extends the verification techniques to the realm of resource allocation. The example presented in this chapter is Hoare's structured paging system. The complexity of Hoare's system approaches that of a real-world problem. The code for Hoare's system is presented in Appendix B.

Chapter 8 attempts to tie up the loose ends, or at least point them out as topics for future research.

Appendix A should be of interest to those desiring to use temporal logic. It contains the proofs of a number of simple theorems that I have found useful during my research.

Note that the algorithms and proofs of this thesis are presented in the following order: first the algorithm, and then the specification and proof. This should not suggest that programs be written and verified in that order. If the programs in this thesis were being written for the first time, instead of being taken from the literature, then both the programs and the specifications would be developed simultaneously, with at least the first steps of the proof in mind at all times.

Chapter 2
Programming Environment

A major tenet of this thesis is that parallel programs written in a well-structured manner can be verified. There are many structured parallel languages being developed or in use (for example, Algol68, Concurrent Pascal, and Ada). The programming language that we present in this chapter and use in this thesis is called VALET (Verification and Algorithm Language Especially for Theses). VALET is based upon Pascal, but it has extensions to permit concurrency, synchronization, and verification. Processes and monitors provide concurrency and synchronization. Auxiliary variables and auxiliary functions aid verification. We assume that the reader is familiar with Pascal and with the notion of monitors.

The language VALET provides a uniform means to describe the various algorithms presented later in this thesis. Using VALET, rather than some implemented language, allows us to take liberties with the language syntax when it is convenient. We do not want to clutter the discussion with the implementation details of fifo queues, multisets, and other low-level data abstractions; VALET includes these constructs as predefined types. It is not intended that VALET be implemented. Therefore, we can use constructs that are not efficient to implement, but are easier to read or to verify than similar constructs in conventional languages. For example, we use diagrams to describe the interconnection of modules, when diagrams present that information more clearly than does code.

2.1. Pascal-like Constructs

The basic structure of VALET is similar to that of Pascal. A VALET program consists of a series of statements and comments. The statements are built from reserved words, identifiers, and operators. Comments are strings enclosed in braces. There are two major syntactic differences between Pascal and VALET. In VALET, the body of a compound statement ends with a keyword rather than being delimited by a begin-end block, and there are no statement-separators in VALET that correspond to semicolons in Pascal.

The language VALET has two conditional statements (if and case) and three iteration statements (while, for, and loop). We specify the syntax of these five constructs in Figure 2.1-1. The curly braces indicate that the construct they enclose can be repeated zero or more times. Constructs enclosed in square brackets can occur zero or one times.

<if-statement> ::=
      if *<boolean-expression>* then
         <statement-list>
      { elseif *<boolean-expression>* then
         <statement-list> }
      [else
         <statement-list>]
      fi

<case-statement> ::=
      case *<expression>* of
         { *<label>*:
            <statement-list> }
         [else:
            <statement-list>]
      end case

<while-statement> ::=
      while *<boolean-expression>* do
         <statement-list>
      od

<for-statement> ::=
      for *<variable>* $\in$ *<set-or-subrange>* do
         <statement-list>
      od

<loop-statement> ::=
      loop
         <statement-list>
      end loop

Figure 2.1-1
Pascal-like Constructs in VALET

2.2. Processes and Monitors

Besides ending with keywords, the first four statements differ slightly from their Pascal counterparts. The else-clause of the case statement receives control when no label matches the value of the tested expression. The variable in the for statement can range over finite sets and subranges. The loop statement corresponds to the Pascal statement

while *true* do begin · · · end.

Procedures and functions in VALET are similar to their Pascal counterparts. There are, however, three minor differences. In VALET, procedures end with end procedure, functions end with end function, and functions return values by executing a return statement. (The return statement will always be the last statement of a function; this avoids the issue of multiple exit points in a function.) In VALET, procedures and functions follow the scope rules of Pascal except when they occur in monitors. Procedures and functions of monitors are visible only to processes or monitors given the right to access them.

VALET extends Pascal in other directions. VALET has a number of useful types that are not included in Pascal: word (a machine word used in describing a paging system), queue, item (a data element with unspecified structure used to represent the contents of a message), history (an unbounded sequence, with the concatenation operator @). VALET allows constants to be specified by compile-time expressions. Arrays in VALET are initialized as shown in Figure 2.1–2. The index variable of the array in such an initialization need not be declared. Two operators $\oplus$ and $\ominus$ are provided to represent addition and subtraction modulo a constant; the modulus is specified in the declaration of the variables involved.

2.2. Processes and Monitors

We model parallel programs as a set of interacting processes and monitors. A *process* is an active program component, in essence a program in itself or a procedure with its own program counter. A *monitor* is a data abstraction with synchronization. Processes and monitors can be combined into modules. The binding together of monitors and processes is static, and it is defined in diagrams associated with the programs. These diagrams specify the monitors that each process (and monitor) can access and the services available to the calling module. Figure 2.2–1 shows a hypothetical system in which processes A, B, and C can send information to the buffer D by executing a *put* operation. Processes E and F can receive information from the buffer by executing a *get* operation. The supervising process G can call a *status* function to obtain

```
type
      accounts = 1..100
var
      BankBalance: array [accounts] of real
begin
      {initialize balances to zero}
      ∀ i ∈ accounts (BankBalance[i] := 0)
end
```

Figure 2.1-2
Array Initialisation

2.2. *Processes and Monitors*

statistics on the buffer's operation. The testing process H can execute both *put* and *get* procedures. These name-module bindings could be expressed in the system's code. For the purpose of describing the system to the reader, however, diagrams are more convenient.

It is often convenient to have levels of abstraction between the high-level program and the low-level processes and monitors. The **module** provides that intermediate-level abstraction. The **module** construct in VALET performs two functions. It serves as an information hiding device by associating monitors, processes, and lower-level modules into a distinct entity as seen from the outside, and it serves as a means for renaming by providing a mapping between **module-procedures** and lower-level **monitor-procedures** (as well as between high-level and low-level **module-procedures**). Modules provide no synchronization, perform no initialization, and create no new functions. In Figures 2.2–2 and 2.2–3 we show an example of a module. The access privileges inside and outside the module are specified by system diagrams. The mapping between the module- and the monitor-procedures is included in the code.

Monitors

Both Brinch Hansen [6] and Hoare [18] developed the notion of a monitor. A monitor consists of a collection of data structures and a set of procedures that operate on these structures. Data internal to a monitor are invisible from outside the monitor; such data can be accessed by external processes only through the specified *visible* procedures. The visible procedures of a monitor are executed in *mutual exclusion*: only one process can be executing any procedure of a given monitor at a time. Processes attempting to access a monitor that is already in use are forced to wait. Monitors also have a variable initialization section, delimited by **begin** and **end**. Initialization occurs before any external access to the monitor is permitted.

A process may have to wait before executing a monitor procedure, or it can wait as a result of having executed a **wait** statement. A process (or monitor) executing a procedure of a monitor X is said to *own* X. If the calling process (or monitor) is suspended because it executed a **wait** statement within X then that calling process (or monitor) is said to have *released* X. The monitor X is also released when the calling process (or monitor) finishes the execution of the called procedure. These are the only two conditions under which a monitor is released. In particular, monitor calls nested within other monitor calls do not release the outer monitor, even if the inner call is suspended.

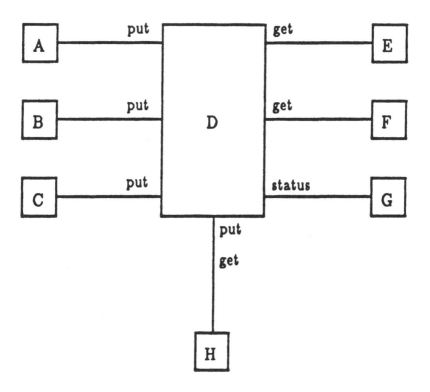

Figure 2.2–1
A Buffer System

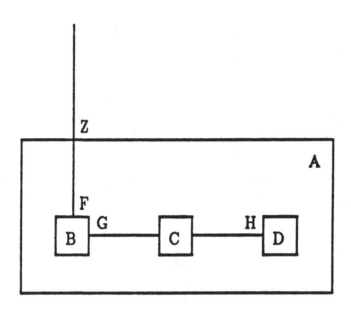

Figure 2.2-2
Module Procedures

A: module

    B: monitor

        . . .

        visible procedure $F(x)$

        . . .

        visible procedure $G(a,b,c)$

        . . .

    end monitor

    C: monitor

        . . .

        visible procedure $H(u,v)$

        . . .

    end monitor

    D: process

        . . .

        $B.G(d,e,f)$

        . . .

        $C.H(w,y)$

        . . .

    end process

    procedure $Z(x) \equiv B.F(x)$

end module

Figure 2.2–3
Module Procedures

2.2. Processes and Monitors

Figure 2.2–4 is an example of a monitor for a stack that is shared among a set of processes. Processes that use the shared stack are able to execute only *push* and *pop* operations. There is no direct way for a calling processes to determine how many items are needed to fill or empty the stack. No process can see how many elements there are in the stack.

When a process P executes a *push* operation, it must first gain ownership of the monitor. When that ownership is granted, no other process can execute a *push* or *pop* until P releases the monitor The first statement within the *push* procedure is a wait until the stack is not full. Upon executing this wait statement, P releases the monitor and waits. When P regains the monitor it is guaranteed that the stack is not full. The top pointer is incremented and the data is stored. When the procedure terminates, the monitor is released.

Two queues of processes that are contending for a monitor are maintained, One for *external waits* and one for *internal waits*. Processes on the external queue are waiting to begin executing a monitor procedure. Process on the internal queue have begun to execute a procedure, but have suspended themselves at a wait statement. When the monitor is released, the wait condition of each process on the internal queue is checked. If any of the conditions are true, then one of the processes with a true condition is allowed to resume control of the monitor. That choice is made fairly, so that no process is forever denied ownership of the monitor. If no process on the internal queue is able to proceed, then a process on the external queue is chosen (fairly).

Monitors in VALET differ from conventional monitors in two ways. In VALET monitors, wait statements have conditions that are boolean expressions. Other languages have a special type of variable called a *condition variable*. In these languages, *wait* statements place the calling process on a queue associated with the condition variable. They also have a *signal* operation that removes a process from a condition queue. (Howard [20, 21] discusses the verification of monitors that use condition variables, *wait* operations, and *signal* operations.) In VALET wait statements, the use of a boolean expression simplifies the verification rules for monitors. The second difference is that wait statements in VALET always release the monitor, regardless of the truth value of the condition. Most other forms of monitors release control only when the condition is false. For the purposes of verification, we make assertions about a monitor that are guaranteed to be true when no process owns the monitor. Our form of the wait statement strengthens the range of these assertions.

Some systems contain multiple copies of the same kind of monitor. In that case we shall define a template for the monitor. Such a construct is called a monitor template. Instances of this template can be declared separately or collected into an array. Figure 2.2–4 specified a shared-stack monitor. If we

```
SharedStack: monitor

constant
     size = 100
var
     stack: array [ 1..size ] of integer
     top: 0..size

function full: boolean
begin
     return ( top = size )
end function

function empty: boolean
begin
     return ( top = 0 )
end function

visible procedure push ( x: integer )
begin
     wait ( ~ full )
     top := top + 1
     stack [ top ] := x
end procedure

visible procedure pop ( var x: integer )
begin
     wait ( ~ empty )
     x := stack [ top ]
     top := top - 1
end procedure

begin
     top := 0
end monitor
```

Figure 2.2–4
Shared Stack Monitor

2.2. *Processes and Monitors*

desire one hundred of these stacks, we would write the code shown in Figure 2.2–5.

Each element of *StackArray* (*StackArray*[1], *StackArray*[2], and so on) is an independent monitor. We write a *pop* operation on the third stack as

$$StackArray[3].pop(x).$$

VALET also allows for both procedure template and module template statements.

There are a few more features of VALET to be discussed. Most concern program verification and are presented in Section 5.1. Chapter 7 introduces *shared data* for the discussion of Hoare's structured paging system.

StackTemplate: monitor template

   . . .

     { *same as SharedStack* }

   . . .

end monitor template

StackArray: array [*1..100*] of *StackTemplate*

Figure 2.2–5
One Hundred Shared Stacks

Chapter 3

Verification

This chapter presents a brief history of program verification. The discussion is not intended to cover all of the literature on the subject, but rather the works that lead directly to the techniques presented in this thesis.

When we verify that a program is correct, we prove that the instructions of the program meet a logical specification of that program. A proof is valid only in the context of the program's implementation; certain assumptions are made as to how the program is implemented, scheduled, and executed. These assumptions are embodied in the set of axioms and inference rules that describe the programming language and the system.

Two kinds of properties, *safety* and *liveness*, are important for parallel systems. Safety properties have the form "bad things will not happen." They are analogous to partial correctness and are expressed by invariant assertions and pre- and post-conditions. Invariant assertions are logical statements that must be satisfied by the system state at all times. Pre- and post-conditions relate the state of a program before the execution of a statement to the state after the termination of the statement.

Liveness properties have the form "good things will happen." They include termination requirements in sequential programs and recurrent properties in non-terminating programs. (Operating systems, for example, should not terminate, but they are intended to repeatedly service requests.) Aside from sequential termination, there has been little work on the verification of liveness properties.

Section 3.1 describes the foundation of program verification: the method developed by Floyd for assigning meaning to programs. Section 3.2 presents an overview of Hoare's axiom system for proving safety properties of programs. Manna and Pnueli extended Hoare's system to prove liveness properties, and that work is discussed in Section 3.3. These first three sections deal with sequential programs. Section 3.4 describes the technique of Owicki and Gries for proving parallel programs. Section 3.5 surveys some existing systems that use the notion of modularity to specify and verify programs.

3.1. Floyd

3.1. Floyd

This thesis follows a verification tradition that began with Floyd's inductive assertion method for sequential programs [9]. Floyd models programs as flowcharts: the nodes represent program statements, and the arcs represent the flow of control. The approach attaches logical assertions to the arcs. The assertion for an arc must be true whenever control passes over that arc.

Floyd's flowcharts consist of five constructs: start, halt, assignment, test, and merge (two control paths merging into one path). The assertion attached to the arc coming from the start command is called the *entry-condition* of the program. It represents the information that can be assumed about the initial state of the program's variables. The assertion attached to the arc leading to the halt command is the *exit-condition* of the program. These conditions are interpreted as follows. When a program begins execution with its entry-condition being true, it is guaranteed that the exit-condition will be true if and when the execution terminates. Floyd gives rules for what assertions can be attached to a given arc. Figure 3.1–1 presents a proof of a simple program that adds n numbers, where $n > 0$.

Let command c have entrances $a_1, a_2, \ldots, a_k$ and exits $b_1, b_2, \ldots, b_l$. The assertion attached to entrance a_i is denoted P_i, and the assertion attached to exit b_j is denoted Q_j. The P assertions are called the entry-conditions of command c. The Q assertions are called the exit-conditions of c. To verify the exit-conditions of c in terms of the entry-conditions, we must show the following: if control enters c by way of some entrance a_i with P_i true, and if control exits c by way of some exit b_j, then Q_j must be true. Floyd gives rules, called *verification conditions*, for deriving the exit-condition of each construct based upon its entry-condition.

These entry- and exit-conditions are safety properties of the program. They specify what will happen *if* something does happen. Floyd also describes a technique for proving that a program will terminate; a liveness property. In this technique a function, called a *W-function*, is selected. The W-function maps the set of program variables to a well-ordered set W. (If W is ordered, and if there are no infinitely decreasing sequences in W, then W is well-ordered.) We prove that a program terminates by showing (for all arcs) that every time control passes over an arc, the value of the W-function decreases.

Floyd sets the cornerstone for verification with the idea of attaching assertions to statements to describe the behavior of the statements. The next section discusses Hoare's axiom system for deriving verification conditions.

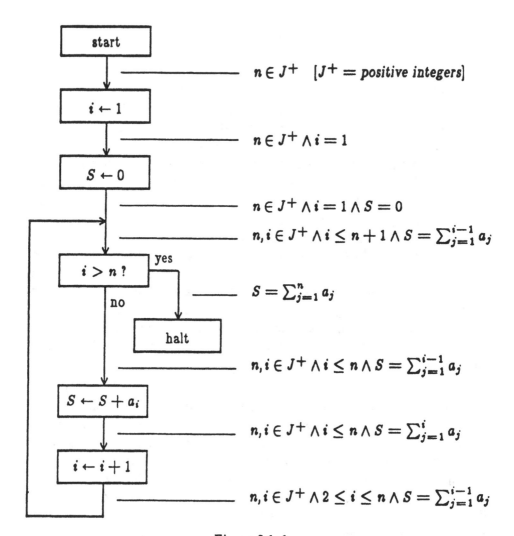

Figure 3.1–1
Flowchart of Program to Compute $\sum_{j=1}^{n} a_j$

3.2. Hoare

Hoare [15] describes an axiomatic basis for proving safety properties of sequential programs. The programs are written using an Algol-like syntax. Two assertions are associated with each instruction. These assertions represent the *pre-condition* and the *post-condition* of the associated statement (analogous to Floyd's entry- and exit-conditions).

If S is a program and if P and Q are the pre- and post-conditions of S, we write

$$\{P\}S\{Q\}$$

to mean that if P is true before S executes, and if S terminates, then Q will be true. The assertions P and Q are both truth functions on the domains of the program variables. (Originally, Hoare wrote $P\{S\}Q$ rather than $\{P\}S\{Q\}$. Pascal uses set-brackets to delimit comments, and the notation $\{P\}S\{Q\}$ follows that convention.)

Hoare gives four rules for deriving the pre- and post-conditions of a program statement. They are

$$\{P_f^x\}\, x := f \,\{P\} \qquad\qquad\qquad assignment$$

$$\frac{\{P'\}S\{Q'\}, P \supset P', Q' \supset Q}{\{P\}S\{Q\}} \qquad\qquad consequence$$

$$\frac{\{P_1\}S_1\{P_2\}, \{P_2\}S_2\{P_3\}, \cdots, \{P_n\}S_n\{P_{n+1}\}}{\{P_1\} \text{ begin } S_1; S_2; \cdots; S_n \text{ end } \{P_{n+1}\}} \qquad composition$$

$$\frac{\{P \wedge B\}S\{P\}}{\{P\} \text{ while } B \text{ do } S \,\{P \wedge \sim B\}} \qquad\qquad iteration.$$

The formula P_f^x represents assertion P with all free occurrences of x replaced by f. Three of these rules are inference rules, which take the form

$$\frac{a_1, a_2, \cdots, a_n}{b}.$$

That is, if $a_1, a_2, \cdots, a_n$ are all true, then b is also true.

Hoare presents, as an example, a program to find the quotient q and remainder r obtained when dividing x by y. All variables in the program represent non-negative integers. The code is shown in Figure 3.2–1.

```
r := x;
q := 0;
while y ≤ r do begin
      r := r-y;
      q := q+1
end
```

Figure 3.2-1

Division by Repeated Subtraction

$\{x \geq 0 \land y > 0\}$
$r := x;$
$\{x = r \land x \geq 0 \land y > 0\}$
$q := 0$
$\{q = 0 \land x = r \land x \geq 0 \land y > 0\}$
$\{x = 0 + r \land r \geq 0 \land q = 0\}$
$\{x = y \times q + r \land r \geq 0\}$
while $y \leq r$ do begin
      $\{x = y \times q + r \land y \leq r \land r \geq 0\}$
      $r := r - y;$
      $\{x = y \times (q + 1) + r \land r \geq 0\}$
      $q := q + 1$
      $\{x = y \times q + r \land r \geq 0\}$
end
$\{x = y \times q + r \land y > r \geq 0\}$

Figure 3.2-2

Proof of Division Algorithm

3.3. Manna and Pnueli

In order to prove that q and r have the correct values when the program terminates, we show that the equality

$$x = y \times q + r \qquad\qquad (I)$$

is invariant over the execution of the while loop. If we assume that I is a loop-invariant, then we can reason as follows. If the program terminates, it can do so only by failing the while test. The while test cannot affect the value of any of the program variables; therefore, if the program terminates, it does so with $x = y \times q + r$.

To prove that I is a loop-invariant, we first show that I holds before the first execution of the loop. We then prove that if we assume that I is true at the beginning of the loop-body, then I must be true at the end of the loop-body. The iteration inference rule then allows us to conclude that

$$x = y \times q + r \quad \wedge \quad y > r \geq 0$$

at the end of the loop (and at the end of the program). The proof is outlined in Figure 3.2–2.

Hoare provides no mechanism for proving termination. The next section describes Manna and Pnueli's axiomatic approach to proving termination.

3.3. Manna and Pnueli

Just as Hoare extends Floyd's technique by providing an axiom system for proving the safety aspects of verification, Manna and Pnueli [29] extend Floyd's work by providing an axiom system for proving termination. Their technique is built upon Floyd's W-functions; but rather than requiring a separate proof of termination, they present rules for unifying the safety and liveness proofs.

Hoare's rules are of the form

$$\{p(\overline{x})\} S \{q(\overline{x})\}.$$

In other words, if p is true of the variables $\overline{x}$ before S is executed, and if S terminates, then q is true of $\overline{x}$ afterwards. Manna and Pnueli extend this notation to

$$< p(\overline{x}) \mid S \mid q(\overline{x}, \overline{x}') > .$$

We read this as follows: for every $\overline{x}$, where $\overline{x}$ is the initial value of the variables, if $p(\overline{x})$ holds prior to the execution of S, then S shall terminate with $q(\overline{x}, \overline{x}')$

3.3. *Manna and Pnueli*

true, where $\bar{x}'$ is the resulting value of the variables. The statement "S will terminate" would be written as

$$< p(\bar{x}) \mid S \mid true > .$$

Manna and Pnueli present ten rules for deriving the pre- and post-conditions for the usual set of program statements. They prove termination by using *well-founded sets* and *convergence functions* (analogous to Floyd's well-ordered sets and W-functions). The following quotation describes the use of convergence functions in proving the termination of a *while* statement:

> Consider a general while statement
>
> $$L: \text{while } t(\bar{x}) \text{ do } B.$$
>
> The termination property of such a while statement is proved by establishing a *convergence function* $u(\bar{x})$ mapping the program variable's domain X into a range W. W is required to be a well-founded set with respect to the relation $\prec$, i.e., allows no infinitely descending sequence $w_1, w_2, \ldots$ such that $w_i \in W$ and $w_i \succ w_{i+1}$ for each i. Such $u(\bar{x})$ is a convergence function for the block B if on subsequent executions of B the value of $u(\bar{x})$ decreases. Thus if we can prove, using our inference rules that
>
> (*) $< p(\bar{x}) \wedge t(\bar{x}) \mid B \mid p(\bar{x}') \wedge u(\bar{x}) \succ u(\bar{x}') >$
>
> this ensures that the while statement having B as its body converges [29].

Nested loops require an extension to (*) so that inner loops can take into account the state of outer loops.

(**) $< p(\bar{x}) \wedge t(\bar{x}) \mid B \mid p(\bar{x}') \wedge q(\bar{x}, \bar{x}') \wedge u(\bar{x}) \succ u(\bar{x}') >$

The formula $p(\bar{x})$ is the loop invariant and $q(\bar{x}, \bar{x}')$ contains information about the convergence of any outer loops.

This technique has an advantage over Floyd's approach, because the liveness proof can be done separately, or it can be incorporated with the safety proof.

We have previously discussed verifying only sequential programs. The next section describes the work of Owicki and Gries, which extends verification to the realm of parallel programs.

3.4. Owicki and Gries

Owicki and Gries [33] define an axiom system that is powerful enough to prove safety properties of parallel programs. They also introduce auxiliary variables as an aid to parallel-program verification.

Parallel programs can display complex behavior due to the interactions among processes. Consider the following example given by Owicki [32]:

process1:	process2:
x := 1	x := 2
y := x+1	y := 5+x.

What is the result of executing the two processes in parallel? There are six possible execution sequences, which result in four different values of y (2, 3, 6, 7). Such complexity increases the chance of programmer error. Synchronization is necessary to control such interference. Verification is necessary to guarantee that programs with complex interactions meet their specifications.

Owicki and Gries present two program constructs, originally due to Hoare [16], that model parallelism: the *resource* and the *with* statement. These constructs are stated as follows:

(1) resource r_1 (variable list), $\cdots$, r_m (variable list)
      cobegin S_1 // $\cdots$ // S_n coend

(2) with r when B do S.

In (1), r_i is a set of logically-related, shared variables and $S_1, \ldots, S_n$ are the statements to be executed in parallel. In (2), r is a resource, B is a boolean expression, and S is a statement that uses the variables of r. Only one process is allowed to use a resource at a time. When a process tries to execute a *with* statement, it is delayed until both B is true and no other process has control of r. Each shared variable must be included in one and only one resource. No shared variable can be accessed outside of a *with* statement controlling its resource.

Owicki and Gries discuss two inference rules that describe these two constructs. But even with these additions to Hoare's axioms, the logical system is not strong enough to prove some simple safety properties of parallel programs. To prove a safety property of a parallel program, it is sometimes necessary to add variables that do not affect the original intent of the program, but instead record extra information needed for the proof. Such variables are called *auxiliary variables*. They are used only to reason about the program. Auxiliary

variables can never be used in an assignment to any of the original variables
of the program, or in the tests of the *while* and *if* statements. Thus, they do
not affect the control flow of the program. As a result, auxiliary variables need
not be implemented; statements involving them do not generate object code.

3.5. Modularity

In his 1969 verification paper [15], Hoare discussed the possibility of proving properties of a procedure within a program and then of using these properties to prove facts about the calling program. This proof technique is similar to
the software-design methodologies of *information hiding* and *stepwise refine-
ment*. These methodologies state that a problem should be solved by decomposing it into smaller subproblems. The subproblems are solved independently,
possibly by further decomposition. The structure of the program is kept simple
by hiding the implementation details of one subproblem from the solution to
another subproblem. This allows equivalent solutions for a given subproblem
to be substituted for each other without affecting the correctness of the solution of the entire problem. Similarly, Hoare's proposal suggests that the proof
of a procedure can be independent of the proofs of other parts of the whole
program. This would allow one proof of the given procedure to be substituted
for another proof of the same procedure without affecting the correctness of
the proof of the entire program.

This concept of decomposing a system and its proof is often used in this
thesis. The concept of program modularity has been closely examined in
recent years, and this section will present an overview of four approaches to
modularization: Mesa, Alphard, CLU, and algebraic specification.

Mesa

In Mesa [11, 31], *modules* provide the capability for partitioning a large
system into manageable units. *Modules* represent data abstractions: they consist of a collection of variables and a set of procedures that perform operations
on these variables. The *modules* are intended to be compiled independently.
From our point of view, the most interesting feature of *modules* is that the
internal details of an implementation can be decoupled from the abstract behavior by using two types of *modules*: definitions and implementations.

The definition *modules* define the interface to the data abstraction. They
specify shared data, name visible procedures, and define input/output types.

3.5. Modularity

The definition *modules* do not exist at run time. They are used for compile-time type checking across *module* boundaries.

Each definition *module* must be associated with an implementation *module*. Types are checked to guarantee that the functions being called and variables being accessed in the definition *module* correctly correspond to the implemented functions and data stuctures.

Alphard

The Alphard [14, 42] data-abstraction mechanism is called a *form*. The primary goal for the *form*'s design is to permit the localization of information concerning a user-defined abstraction. It is designed to localize both the verification of the abstraction and the effects of modifications made to the implementation of the abstraction.

A *form* is composed of a specification section and an implementation section. The specification section lists what properties the *form* has, what functions it makes available, the initial values of its components, and assertions describing the operation of the *form*. The implementation section defines how the visible data structures and the functions are implemented.

Alphard allows for the specification of *form* invariants and of pre- and post-assertions for the *form* functions. The *form* can be verified by showing that the pre- and post-assertions for each implemented function are valid, and that the assertions for the implemented version of the *form* correctly correspond to the assertions for the abstract version of the *form*.

CLU

The language CLU [24] provides three types of abstractions: data, procedural, and control. Data abstractions are called *clusters*; they represent data objects and associated operations that characterize the behavior of these objects. A procedural abstraction performs a computation on a set of input objects and produces a set of output objects. Procedural abstractions are implemented by procedures. A control abstraction defines a method for sequencing arbitrary actions; it is a generalization of the iteration constructs of other languages.

Useful abstractions are stored in the CLU library. The library supports incremental program development; it encourages programers to write and test

3.5. *Modularity*

one abstraction at a time, and to share that work with others. The information in the library permits the separate compilation of single modules including complete type checking of external references. For each abstraction in the library, there is a description unit that contains all system-maintained information about that abstraction. Included in the description unit are modules that implement the data abstraction and that interface specifications containing the information needed for type checking. Internal/external names are bound using an association list, which maps names to description units.

Algebraic Specification

The previous three subsections have discussed programming languages that use modularization. The abstraction technique allows for the specification of modules in some terms other than a sample implementation. Alphard further exploits abstraction by incorporating verification assertions in the modules. All of these languages define the abstractions by stating what data is visible and what functions can be called. The algebraic specification technique developed by Guttag, Horowitz, and Musser [13] is different. It is a specification language, rather than a programming language. It defines the effects of executing a given operation in terms of the other operations of the module.

As a program is developed using this technique, the levels of abstraction are described algebraically; the operations on the data type are related by equalities. As the code is written, it must be shown to satisfy the algebraic specification. Guttag, Horowitz, and Musser present, as an example, an unbounded-stack data type. To verify that the stack is implemented correctly, lower-level data types must be defined (algebraically). The stack is then implemented in terms of these primitive data types. They then prove that the specification of each high-level operation is satisfied by the implementation.

> One of the most important aspects of the proof technique used to prove correctness of algebraically specified data types is that proofs are factored into levels corresponding to the implementation levels. To prove the correctness of a data type implemented in terms of other data types, we need to rely only on the axiomatic specifications of the other data types, *not* on their implementations [13].

3.5. Modularity

Modularity and Verification

The data abstraction techniques described above are useful for writing large complex programs; they allow smaller parts of the problem to be solved independently. In this thesis, we exploit this modularity in two ways. First, scope rules allow us to simplify our proofs of the individual modules, because many possible interactions and conflicts cannot occur because the modules are independent. Second, hiding the details of the modules simplifies the proof of the higher-level constructs; their proofs do not involve verifying code, but rather involve reasoning with combinations of logical assertions.

Chapter 4
Temporal Logic

Temporal logic provides operators for reasoning about program computations. A computation is a sequence of states that can arise during program execution. Informally, the first state in a computation represents the present, and subsequent states represent the future. Computations are not restricted to starting at the beginning of the program, so a future state in one computation can be the present state in another.

4.1. Introduction

The version of temporal logic used in this thesis was developed by Pnueli [10, 37, 38, 39], and is further described by Lamport [23]. Hughes and Cresswell [22] provide an excellent introduction to the field of modal* logic, of which temporal logic is a part. Temporal logic has three modal operators. The two used most often in this thesis are □ (henceforth) and ◇ (eventually). The formula □P (henceforth P) means that P is true for all points in the computation. The formula ◇P (eventually P) means that there is some point in the computation at which P is true. The operators □ and ◇ are duals:

$$\Box P \equiv \sim \Diamond \sim P.$$

When we say that a temporal formula is true for a program, we mean that it is true for all computations of that program.

If we informally interpret the first state of a computation as representing the present and the subsequent states as representing the future, then we can think of the modal operators as quantifying over time. Under this interpretation, □P means that P is true now and will remain true forever. The formula ◇P states that either P is true now or it will be true at some time in the future.

Temporal operators can be used to express both safety and liveness properties. For example, program termination is a liveness property, and it can be expressed by the formula

$$at\, P \quad \supset \quad \Diamond \; after\, P,$$

where *at P* and *after P* are assertions that are true of states in which control is (respectively) at the beginning or end of the program. An example of a safety

---

*The adjective *modal* is explained in Section 4.5 on the history of temporal logic.

4.1. Introduction

property is an inductive assertion: an assertion that will remain true if it ever becomes true. To state that I is an inductive assertion, we would write

$$\Box(I \supset \Box I).$$

Combinations of the two modal operators are also useful. For example, the formula $\Box \Diamond P$ (*infinitely often* P) implies that there are an infinite number of future states in which P is true. (To understand this interpretation, note that $\Diamond P$ implies that P will be true in some future state. The formula $\Box \Diamond P$ states that this will always be true. In particular, if P ever becomes false, it is guaranteed to become true again at some later state. Therefore, P must be true infinitely often.) The $\Box \Diamond$ modality is especially useful for stating recurring properties of a program. For example, in order to prove that a bounded buffer operates correctly, we shall want to show that

$$\Box \Diamond (the\ buffer\ is\ not\ full).$$

The dual of infinitely often is $\Diamond \Box$ (*eventually henceforth*). The formula $\Diamond \Box P$ means that there is some state after which P remains true forever. An example of the use of this modality concerns program deadlock. Deadlock occurs when each process in a system is waiting for some other process to release a resource. We can state that deadlock is inevitable by the formula

$$\Diamond \Box (all\ processes\ are\ waiting).$$

Pnueli's temporal logic system contains one additional modal operator: $\bigcirc$ (*next*). The formula $\bigcirc P$ means that P is true in the second state of the computation. We shall use the $\bigcirc$ operator to derive temporal theorems, but we shall not use it for reasoning about programs, so as to avoid discussing the exact time scale of our programs.

A *modality* is defined as any unbroken sequence of zero or more modal operators. The *degree* of a modality is the number of operators in the sequence. If there are no modal operators in a formula (degree zero), then that formula refers only to the first state in the computation: the present. The first degree modalities are *henceforth*, *eventually*, and *next*. The modalities of degree two we have discussed are *infinitely often* and *eventually henceforth*. We show in Section 4.3 that within Pnueli's axiom system, any modality that does not contain the $\bigcirc$ operator and that has degree greater than two is equivalent to a modality of degree one or degree two.

4.2. Syntax

The specification of a logical system has four parts: a list of *primitive symbols* (alternatively this can be a list of primitive symbols and a second list of symbols defined in terms of the primitive symbols); a set of *formation rules* that specify which sentences on the alphabet of primitive symbols are *well-formed formulas* (wffs); a selected set of wffs, known as *axioms*; and a set of *inference rules* that permit operations on the axioms and those wffs that have been generated by previous applications of the inference rules. The wffs obtained by applying inference rules are known as *theorems*. If *A* is an axiom or a theorem then we write $\vdash A$.

The definition of Pnueli's temporal system **DX** follows.

Primitive symbols:

$P\,Q\,R\,S\ldots$ atomic predicates (uninterpreted symbols)

The usual logical operators:

$\sim$	logical negation
$\vee \wedge \supset \equiv$	logical and, or, implication, equivalence
$(\,)$	brackets

The modal operators:

□ ◇ ○	henceforth, eventually, next

Formation rules:

1) an atomic predicate is a wff.
2) if α is a wff then so are $\sim(\alpha)$, $\Box(\alpha)$, $\Diamond(\alpha)$, and $\bigcirc(\alpha)$.
3) if α and β are wffs then so are
   $(\alpha \vee \beta)$, $(\alpha \wedge \beta)$, $(\alpha \supset \beta)$, and $(\alpha \equiv \beta)$.

Brackets will not be required when they are redundant. Strictly speaking, only $\sim$, $\vee$, □, and ○ need be primitive operators. The others can be defined in terms of $\sim$, $\vee$, and □.

4.3. Axioms

The axioms of **DX** include the axioms of propositional calculus and the following eight temporal axioms:

$$\Diamond P \equiv \sim\Box\sim P \qquad A0$$
$$\Box(P \supset Q) \supset (\Box P \supset \Box Q) \qquad A1$$
$$\Box P \supset P \qquad A2$$
$$\bigcirc(\sim P) \equiv \sim(\bigcirc P) \qquad A3$$
$$\bigcirc(P \supset Q) \supset (\bigcirc P \supset \bigcirc Q) \qquad A4$$
$$\Box P \supset \bigcirc P \qquad A5$$
$$\Box P \supset \bigcirc\Box P \qquad A6$$
$$\Box(P \supset \bigcirc P) \supset (P \supset \Box P). \qquad A7$$

The system **DX** has three inference rules: *TAU, MP,* and *GEN.*

$$\frac{A \text{ is an instance of a tautology}}{\vdash A} \qquad TAU$$

$$\frac{\vdash A \quad \& \quad \vdash (A \supset B)}{\vdash B} \qquad MP$$

$$\frac{\vdash A}{\vdash \Box A} \qquad GEN$$

Appendix A gives a list of derived theorems for system **DX** . Theorems 1, 1′, 13, and 13′ show that modalities of degree greater than two (that do not involve ○) are equivalent to modalities of degree one or two:

$$\Box\Box P \equiv \Box P \qquad Thm\ 1$$
$$\Diamond\Diamond P \equiv \Diamond P \qquad Thm\ 1'$$
$$\Box\Diamond\Box P \equiv \Diamond\Box P \qquad Thm\ 13$$
$$\Diamond\Box\Diamond P \equiv \Box\Diamond P. \qquad Thm\ 13'$$

Using the above four theorems, we can collapse sequential duplicates of one modal operator (□ or ◇) into a single instance of that operator, and we can remove □ in front of ◇□ and ◇ in front of □◇.

4.4. Semantics

Theorems 2, 2', 18, and 18' specify how the modalities distribute over conjunctions and disjunctions.

$$\square(P \wedge Q) \;\equiv\; (\square P \wedge \square Q) \qquad\qquad Thm\ 2$$
$$\diamond(P \vee Q) \;\equiv\; (\diamond P \vee \diamond Q) \qquad\qquad Thm\ 2'$$
$$\diamond\square(P \wedge Q) \;\equiv\; (\diamond\square P \wedge \diamond\square Q) \qquad\qquad Thm\ 18$$
$$\square\diamond(P \vee Q) \;\equiv\; (\square\diamond P \vee \square\diamond Q) \qquad\qquad Thm\ 18'$$

4.4. Semantics

We define the semantics of temporal logic in a manner similar to Lamport [23]. Informally, a state is the value of the program counter(s) and the values of the program variables. Formally, a *state* is defined to be a truth-valued function on the set of atomic predicates. Lamport explains this definition with the following example.

> Recall that an atomic predicate is an uninterpreted symbol — for example, the string of characters '$a > 0$.' For a program having a variable a, a state z can be interpreted as one in which a has the value 1 if $z('a > 0') =$ true, $z('a > 1') =$ false, $z('a > 2') =$ false, etc. Thus the state of the program is defined by the truth or falsity of each atomic predicate.

The value of a state on a logical combination of predicates is defined in the obvious way. If z is a state and P and Q are predicates then $z(\sim P)$ is defined as $\sim z(P)$ and $z(P \vee Q)$ is $z(P) \vee z(Q)$. These definitions extend to arbitrary logical combinations that use $\sim$, $\vee$, $\wedge$, $\supset$, and $\equiv$.

We must define what a computation is before we can interpret the temporal modalities. A *program model* M is a 4-tuple $(S, \Sigma, \sigma, \Theta)$, where S is a set of states of the program, Σ is a set of execution sequences on the program that meet the *tail-inclusion property* given below, σ is the initial state of the program, and Θ is a subset of Σ called *computations*. Computations are defined below. If s is an *execution sequence* then $s = s_0, s_1, \cdots$. Here s_0 is the initial state of the execution. The first program step from s_0 changes the state to s_1. The second step changes the state to s_2 and so on. If the execution sequence s terminates in n steps, then we represent the execution sequence by repeating the last state: $s_0, s_1, \cdots, s_n, s_n, s_n, \cdots$.

4.4. Semantics

We said before that the present state of one computation can be the future state of some other computation. In order to specify this property, we need a notation to describe the part of an execution sequence that remains after the first few states are removed. We define s^+ to be the sequence obtained by deleting the first element of s:

$$s^+ = s_1, s_2, \cdots.$$

Note that the equality

$$(s^+)_i = s_{i+1}$$

holds for all execution sequences s and all non-negative integers i.

A set of execution sequences Γ has the *tail-inclusion property* if

$$\forall \gamma \in \Gamma \, (\gamma^+ \in \Gamma).$$

In other words, if an execution sequence is in Γ then the *tail* of the sequence is also in Γ. The set Σ is required to have this property. The set of computations Θ is defined as all executions sequences of Σ that have initial state σ and all tails of these sequences, so that the tail-inclusion property holds for Θ as well.

If s is the sequence $s_0, s_1, \cdots$, then we define s^{+n} to be the sequence

$$s_n, s_{n+1}, \cdots.$$

The recursive definition of s^{+n} is

$$s^{+0} = s$$
$$s^{+n} = \left(s^{+(n-1)}\right)^+ \qquad \textit{for } n > 0.$$

Using this notation, the tail-inclusion property implies (by induction) that

$$\forall \gamma \in \Gamma \, (\forall n \geq 0 \, (\gamma^{+n} \in \Gamma)).$$

Given a program model $M = (S, \Sigma, \sigma, \Theta)$ and an assertion A the interpretation for A on a sequence $s \in \Theta$, written A_s, is as follows:

$$\begin{aligned}
&\text{if } A \text{ is an atomic predicate, then } A_s = s_0(A),\\
&\text{if } A = B \vee C, \text{ then } A_s = (B \vee C)_s = B_s \vee C_s,\\
&\text{if } A = B \wedge C, \text{ then } A_s = (B \wedge C)_s = B_s \wedge C_s,\\
&\text{if } A = \sim B, \text{ then } A_s = (\sim B)_s = \sim(B_s),\\
&\text{if } A = \Box B \text{ then } A_s = (\Box B)_s = \forall n \geq 0 \, (B_{s+n}),\\
&\text{if } A = \Diamond B \text{ then } A_s = (\Diamond B)_s = \exists n \geq 0 \, (B_{s+n}),\\
&\text{if } A = \circ B \text{ then } A_s = (\circ B)_s = B_{s+}.
\end{aligned}$$

An assertion A is true for the program model if

$$\forall s \in \Theta \, (A_s)$$

is true: the assertion A is true for all computations of the program.

4.5. History of Temporal Logic

Temporal logic belongs to the class of modal logics. Modal logics distinguish among different types of truth. When reasoning with the system **DX**, we speak of a proposition being true now (modality of degree zero), true henceforth ($\Box$), true eventually ($\Diamond$), and so on. Most modal logics distinguish between propositions that *happen* to be true and propositions that *must* be true. This discussion of modal logic and of the history of temporal logic is based upon the works of Hughes and Cresswell [22] and Rescher and Urquhart [40].

A proposition that is bound to be true is called *necessary*; one that is bound to be false is termed *impossible*. A *contingent* proposition is neither necessary nor impossible. A proposition that is not impossible is *possible*. The exact meaning of "bound to be true (false)" is specified in different ways. The four notions (necessity, impossibility, contingency, and possibility) are said to be *modal* notions. The term *modal* is used because in medieval logic the four notions were thought of as the *modes* in which a proposition can be true or false.

"It is necessary that" is a monadic proposition forming operator on propositions. Such an operator is called a *modal operator*. Hughes and Cresswell abbreviate "it is necessary that" as L and "it is possible that" as M. Necessity and possibility are duals:

$$LP \equiv \, \sim M \sim P.$$

Because the notion "bound to be true (false)" is vague, more than one modal axiom system has been developed. A variety of modal axiom systems can be found in the two sources mentioned above.

The semantic model for modal logic, due to Kripke, allows us to formalize the interpretation of the modalities. Kripke defined a triple (G, K, R), where K is a set of worlds, G is a distinguished member of K, and R is a reflexive relation over K. Atomic predicates are interpreted as true or false for each world. Modal formulas refer to the value of their component predicates on all *accessible* worlds. Accessibility is defined by R. For example, Lp is true on world H, if for all worlds accessible to H, p is true. Different axiom systems develop by further constraining R.

The Kripke model has a direct application to the form of temporal logic that we use. The worlds of K represent the states of a computation. The distinguished world G is the first state of the computation, and R represents the reflexive and transitive relation "now or in the future."

Rescher and Urquhart trace the origins of modal logic back to the ancient Greeks. The Greeks had differing views on how the modalities should be defined. An argument arose between the Stoics and the Megarians as to

4.5. History of Temporal Logic

whether the past should be considered when reasoning about possibility and necessity. The Stoics defined the *possible* as that which is realized at some present-or-future time:

$$MP \quad \text{iff} \quad (\exists t \geq n)T_t(P),$$

where $T_t(P)$ stands for "P is true at time t" and n is "now." They defined the *necessary* as that which is realized at every future time:

$$LP \quad \text{iff} \quad (\forall t \geq n)T_t(P).$$

The Megarians did not allow the modalities to be relative to a "now." Their *possible* is that which is realized at *some* time:

$$MP \quad \text{iff} \quad (\exists t)T_t(P).$$

Necessary to the Megarians was that which is realized at all times:

$$LP \quad \text{iff} \quad (\forall t)T_t(P).$$

Aristotle generally sided with the Stoics, but he did hold the Megarian view when considering the necessary as that which is true all of the time.

The Aristotelian and Stoic logic of temporal relations was further developed by medieval Arabic logicians. In particular, Avicenna developed a highly intricate modal system that would distinguish a variety of truths. Avicenna classed modal propositions into thirteen sorts based upon four basic modal relationships:

$(A/L/B)$ meaning A is necessarily true whenever B is true,
$(A/\forall t/B)$ meaning A is true whenever B is true,
$(A/\exists t/B)$ meaning A is true at some time that B is true,
$(A/M/B)$ meaning A is possible at some time that B is true.

Rescher and Urquhart illustrate some of the variety of these modalities.

> By way of illustration, if A is a categorical proposition "All fire is hot," the Absolute Perpetual modal proposition would read "When there is fire, then it is necessarily hot." The Non-necessary Existential proposition would read "When there is fire it is sometimes hot (but) it is possible that it not be hot." If A is the categorical proposition "Some men are not wise" then the Absolute Perpetual is "When there are men, then there are always some who are not wise," the Special Possible is "When there are men, then possibly some of them are not wise (but) possibly all are wise."

Chapter 5
Techniques

The rest of this thesis is concerned with applying structured verification techniques to two classes of parallel programs: network protocols and resource allocation. In the chapters to come, we verify a number of programs from the literature. The proofs of these programs are important because the programs represent a class of real-world algorithms. The proof of an algorithm, however, is a one-time event; of more lasting value is the technique we develop while proving these programs. This technique can be used to prove the correctness of many other programs.

In Section 5.1, we describe the tools that we use when verifying parallel programs. These tools include inference rules, invariants, commitments, auxiliary variables, and monitor specifications. In Section 5.2, we present eleven verification heuristics as guides in applying the technique.

Verification in this thesis will follow in the style of Hoare and Owicki. The structure of each proof will be modular: the proof will parallel the module structure of the program. The proved properties of lower-level modules, not the implementations, will be used in the higher-level proofs.

In most cases, proofs will follow the same visibility rules that programs follow. A proof of a module cannot refer to any variable local to a submodule, in the same way that the module code cannot access a variable local to a submodule. (For an exception to this rule, see the discussion of private variables in Section 5.1.3.) A proof can refer to the visible procedures of a submodule and any variables in the parameter lists of these procedures.

5.1. Basic Tools

This section discusses the basic tools for verifying safety and liveness properties of parallel programs. Section 5.1.1 presents inference rules for the safety properties of the Pascal-like statements of VALET. Section 5.1.2 describes the various types of invariants used in the thesis; invariants specify safety properties of processes and monitors. We then digress to discuss auxiliary variables (including private variables and history variables) in Section 5.1.3. Section 5.1.4 completes the presentation of safety inference rules with a discussion of wait statements and monitor procedures. Section 5.1.5 discusses liveness inference rules and commitments. Commitments describe conditons that a process (or monitor) guarantees to make true. Section 5.1.6 illustrates how the properties of a process and a monitor are specified.

4.5. History of Temporal Logic

The Latin medievals carried on the interest in modalities. Pseudo-Scotus distinguished four types of necessity: conditional, as-long-as, as-of-now, and for-all-times. Thomas Aquinas and other medieval scholars made the distinction between truths akin to the modern distinction between logical necessity and physical necessity. Interest in such modalities is found as late as William of Ockham.

Hughes and Cresswell find the beginnings of modern modal logic in the work of Hugh MacColl towards the end of the nineteenth century. MacColl speaks of *certainty* and *possibility* but gives no axiom system. In 1912, C. I. Lewis expressed his dissatisfaction with the notion of material implication (the $\supset$ of standard logic). He used an axiom system to describe strict implication $(L(\alpha \supset \beta))$.

Hughes and Cresswell describe a number of axiom systems for modal logic. Two of these systems, S4.3 and D, are commonly used to model time. The system S4.3 models continuous time, where between any two moments there is a third moment. Discrete time is modelled by the system D, which is a forerunner of Pnueli's DX system.

Rescher and Urquhart trace the modern development of temporal logic to three sources: the studies of Stoic logic by Martha Hurst Kneale and Benson Mates and the studies of medieval logic by Ernest Moody, the logical analysis of grammatical tenses by Hans Reichenbach, and the endeavor by the Polish logician Jerzy Los to devise a system of temporal logic. Rescher and Urquhart also present a number of temporal systems that contrast linear, branching, additive, metric, absolute, and relative time.

5.1.2. *Invariants*

5.1.1. Safety Inference Rules—Sequential VALET

The inference rules for the safety properties of parallel programs follow closely those of Owicki [32] and Hoare [15]. The form of each rule is

$$\frac{a_1, a_2, \cdots, a_n}{b}.$$

That is, if $a_1, a_2, \cdots, a_n$ are all true, then b is also true. A safety axiom and the safety inference rules for the sequential VALET statements are shown in Figure 5.1-1. We define the inference rules for the loop and for statements in terms of the inference rules for the corresponding while loops. Similarly, we define the inference rule for the case statement in terms of the inference rule for the if statement. These inference rules form the building blocks from which all of the other safety proofs in this thesis are built.

5.1.2. Invariants

The safety properties of a process (or a monitor) are stated in terms of invariants. There are many flavors of invariants; the most common is a logical statement that must be satisfied by a process at all times. A proof that an assertion is a general invariant requires two steps: first we show that the assertion is implied by the initial conditions, and then we prove for all statements that if the assertion is true before the statement is executed, then the assertion will be true if the statement terminates.

The second type of invariant is the *loop invariant*. In the while-statement inference rule (Figure 5.1-1), P is a loop invariant. It is possible that P may not be true all of the time, but P must be true when the loop is first entered and every time the loop body is finished. To prove that P is a loop invariant, we use a technique that is similar to that used for general invariants: show that P is true the first time the loop is entered, and then show that if P is true at the beginning of the loop body, then it will be true if control reaches the end of the loop body.

The third type of invariant is the *monitor invariant*. A monitor invariant is not necessarily true at all times. A monitor invariant must be true, however, when no process owns the monitor. We prove that an assertion P is a monitor invariant by showing the following: the initialization of the monitor implies P, and if P is true when a process gains control of the monitor, then P will be true when the process releases the monitor. A process can gain control of a monitor at the beginning of a procedure call and after a wait statement.

$$\{P_f^z\}\, x := f\, \{P\} \qquad\qquad\qquad\qquad assignment$$

$$\frac{\{P'\}S\{Q'\},\, P \supset P',\, Q' \supset Q}{\{P\}S\{Q\}} \qquad\qquad consequence$$

$$\frac{\{P_1\}S_1\{P_2\},\, \{P_2\}S_2\{P_3\},\cdots,\{P_n\}S_n\{P_{n+1}\}}{\{P_1\}\ S_1; S_2; \cdots; S_n\ \{P_{n+1}\}} \qquad composition$$

$$\frac{\{P \wedge B\}\, S_1\, \{Q\},\ \{P \wedge \sim B\}\, S_2\, \{Q\}}{\{P\}\text{if } B \text{ then } S_1 \text{ else } S_2 \text{ fi } \{Q\}} \qquad\qquad if$$

$$\frac{\{P \wedge B\}\, S\, \{P\}}{\{P\}\text{ while } B \text{ do } S \text{ od } \{P \wedge \sim B\}} \qquad\qquad while$$

The formula P_f^z stands for the formula P with all free occurrences of x replaced by f.

Figure 5.1–1

Safety Axiom and Inference Rules for Sequential VALET.

5.1.3.   Auxiliary Variables

Similarly, a process releases a monitor at every **wait** statement and at the end of a procedure call.

It is often the case that an invariant describes some facet of a monitor (or process) that is not directly represented in the variables of that monitor (or process). We use auxiliary variables to record the aspects that are not directly represented.

5.1.3. Auxiliary Variables

Auxiliary variables are used to record program information that is needed for a correctness proof, but is not available from the program's code. Auxiliary variables can in no way affect the control flow of the program. As a result, auxiliary variables need not be implemented; statements involving them do not generate object code. Therefore, auxiliary variables can possess properties that would be impractical for normal variables. For example, auxiliary variables can contain an unbounded sequence that records all calls to a procedure, or they can take on the value of integers that are of unbounded magnitude.

Where do we introduce auxiliary variables? In most cases, monitors and process need not retain a history of all of their previous actions in order to perform their function; the state that they maintain is an abstraction of this history. For example, a monitor that implements a semaphore does not need to record the number of P and V operations it has serviced. Instead the monitor's state contains only the number of process allowed to complete a P operation at the current time: zero or one. The proof of a semaphore monitor, however, requires the information that was lost in the abstraction. The proof that only one process is active in its critical region requires showing that the number of completed P operations can exceed by no more than one the number of V operations. Therefore, we use auxiliary variables to record this extra information.

History Variables

One class of auxiliary variables that is useful for reasoning about networks is the class of *history variables*. A history is an unbounded sequence that records the interactions between modules. History variables have frequently been used in reasoning about communication systems [12, 20, 34, 35].

We now introduce some notation for describing histories. Let A and B be arbitrary history sequences. The length of A is denoted by $|A|$. If A has

5.1.3. Auxiliary Variables

elements u, v, y, z then we can write,

$$A = < uvyz > .$$

We denote the ith element of history A by A_i. If $|A| = n$ then we can write

$$A = < a_i >_{i=1}^{n} .$$

We denote concatenation of sequences by juxtaposition:

$$A = < uv >< yz > = < uvyz > .$$

We shall often discuss sequences of repeated messages when referring to the histories of messages sent and received by a network protocol. We define the superscripts $*$ and $+$ as they are defined for regular expressions:

$$A = < a^* > \quad \equiv \quad (\exists k \geq 0)(A = < a^k >)$$
$$A = < a^+ > \quad \equiv \quad (\exists k \geq 1)(A = < a^k >),$$

where $< a^k >$ denotes the message $< a >$ repeated k times. These notations can be combined, for example,

$$A = < a_i^+ >_{i=1}^{n}$$
$$= < a_1^+ >< a_2^+ > \cdots < a_n^+ > .$$

We write $A \preceq B$, if A is an *initial subsequence* of B. This means that $|A| \leq |B|$, and the two sequences are identical in their first $|A|$ elements.

Finally, there are certain temporal assertions about histories that we shall use often when reasoning about liveness. The first is an assertion that the size of a given history will grow without bound. It is abbreviated as $u(A)$, where

$$u(A) = \forall n \, (\Diamond |A| > n),$$

or equivalently

$$u(A) = \forall n \, (\Box(|A| = n \quad \supset \quad \Diamond(|A| > n))).$$

The second assertion states that a particular value occurs an unbounded number of times. Letting $c(A, m)$ be the number of occurrences of m in A, this is stated as

$$uc(A, m) = \forall n \, (\Diamond c(A, m) > n).$$

5.1.3. Auxiliary Variables

Private Variables

Another class of auxiliary variables, called *private variables*, are useful when proving properties concerning a monitor and the processes that call the monitor. It is convenient to state such properties in terms of variables that cannot be changed by any process other than the calling process. A private variable, as defined by Owicki [34], has one instance for each process that uses the monitor. The instance of a private variable that belongs to process P can be changed only by the execution of an operation invoked by P. Thus, a private variable is part of a monitor and can be used in assertions about that monitor. Because each instance can be modified by only one process, a private variable will not change between invocations of the monitor and can be considered as "local" to the calling process. In this sense, private variables violate the visibility rules for monitor variables. In general, monitor variables are not visible to calling processes, but a private variable that belongs to a process is visible to that process.

In Chapter 2, we defined a shared stack monitor. The code for that monitor is repeated in Figure 5.1-2. Suppose that there are three process that can call the shared stack: A, B, and C. Furthermore, suppose that we wish to prove that the current contents of the stack consists of exactly those elements pushed by some process and not popped by any process. We declare two private variables *in* and *out* of type multiset. (A multiset—or bag—is analogous to a set, but elements can appear more than once.) There are three copies of each private variable (one for each calling process): $in[A]$, $in[B]$, $in[C]$, $out[A]$, $out[B]$, and $out[C]$. These private variables are local to the monitor, but each can be modified only by the corresponding calling process. The revised *push* and *pop* procedures are shown in Figure 5.1-3. In the program, we use the auxiliary variable id to represent the identifier of the calling process.

If we let *StackContents* represent the multiset of all the elements in the stack, then the desired monitor invariant is stated as

$$StackContents = in[A] + in[B] + in[C] - out[A] - out[B] - out[C],$$

where $+$ indicates multiset union and $-$ indicates multiset difference.

```
SharedStack: monitor

constant
     size = 100
var
     stack: array [1..size] of integer
     top: 0..size

function full: boolean
begin
     return ( top = size )
end function

function empty: boolean
begin
     return ( top = 0 )
end function

visible procedure push ( x: integer )
begin
     wait ( ~ full )
     top := top + 1
     stack [ top ] := x
end procedure

visible procedure pop ( var x: integer )
begin
     wait ( ~ empty )
     x := stack [ top ]
     top := top - 1
end procedure

begin
     top := 0
end monitor
```

Figure 5.1–2
Shared Stack Monitor

```
var in, out:  private multiset

visible procedure push( x: integer)
begin
      wait ( ~ full)
      top := top + 1
      stack [ top ]  := x
      in [ id ]  := in [ id ]  + x
end procedure

visible procedure pop( var x: integer)
begin
      wait ( ~ empty)
      x := stack [ top ]
      out [ id ]  := out [ id ]  + x
      top := top - 1
end.
```

The + operator represents multiset union.

Figure 5.1–3
Revised Push and Pop Procedures

5.1.4. Safety Properties of Parallel VALET

In this section we discuss the safety axiom for the **wait** statement, how to specify the safety properties of the body of a monitor procedure, and the safety inference rule for a monitor call.

The monitor invariant is the key feature of the safety specification of a monitor. It is true whenever a module assumes control of the monitor, and it must be re-established before the monitor is released. Throughout this section, I will represent the monitor invariant. Note that the same invariant is referred to in all discussions in this section.

The **wait** statement is used within a monitor to guarantee that some condition is true before proceeding with a computation. The safety inference rule for the **wait** statement must provide for a change in the state of the monitor between the time a process releases the monitor and the time that the same process resumes control of the monitor. The **wait** statement safety axiom is

$$\{I \wedge V\} \text{ wait}(B) \{I \wedge V \wedge B\}, \qquad\qquad \textit{wait}$$

where V is an assertion that refers only to private variables of the calling process. Non-private monitor variables could have been changed by other processes during the **wait**, but they must still satisfy the monitor invariant.

A monitor call has pre- and post-assertions, just as other statements of VALET do. These assertions can refer only to private variables of the caller and parameters of the call. We prove the safety properties of a monitor procedure body as follows. Upon entry to the procedure I is true, because I is true whenever control is assumed within a monitor. In addition, we assume that P is true; the calling process must make that guarantee. We must then prove using the other safety inference rules that I is true before each **wait** statement and that both I and Q are true before exiting the procedure. In other words, we must show that

$$\{I \wedge P\} < body > \{I \wedge Q\}$$

is valid for the body of the monitor procedure.

Having proved the safety properties of the procedure body, we can state the inference rule for a call to that monitor procedure:

$$\frac{\{I \wedge P\} < body > \{I \wedge Q\}}{\{P\} < call > \{Q\}}. \qquad\qquad \textit{monitor call}$$

We assume that the appropriate actual parameters are substituted for the formal parameters in the call.

5.1.5.   Commitments and Liveness Inference Rules

Liveness properties are specified by temporal logic assertions called *commitments*. Commitments describe conditions that a module causes to become true. Verifying that a process (or monitor) satisfies its liveness specifications requires reasoning based on assumptions about the liveness properties of each of its component statements. We assume that processes execute *fairly*; each process makes progress unless it is *blocked*. The unblockable actions consist of evaluating an expression and performing an assignment. Both executing a wait statement and calling a monitor procedure are blockable actions. More precisely, let s be an unblockable action in the program. Let "at s" be the assertion that s is ready to be executed, and "*after s*" be the assertion that control has finished s. Our basic liveness assumption can be expressed in temporal logic by

$$\text{at } s \quad \supset \quad \Diamond \text{ after } s.$$

Fairness for monitor calls and wait statements is described below.

In Chapter 7, we shall reason about shared variables. For the sake of simplicity, we shall define a set of atomic operations on each shared object. These atomic operations will be guaranteed to terminate; therefore, our basic liveness assumption will hold for these operations as well.

Starting from these assumptions about program actions, we can derive rules for proving liveness properties of more complex statements. For example, consider a program statement of the form

$$\text{loop } S \text{ end loop,}$$

where S is a statement list that consists of only unblockable actions. For such a statement, we want to prove that

$$\text{at } S \quad \supset \quad \Box\Diamond \text{at } S.$$

That is, control will infinitely often be at the beginning of S.

We specify liveness properties with the following liveness-inference schema.

$$\text{at } S \quad \supset \quad live(S).$$

Where S is a statement list and $live(S)$ is an assertion describing the liveness properties of S. The live assertions for the sequential **VALET** statements are presented in Figure 5.1-4.

$$live(L: \quad x := e):$$
$$\diamond(after\ L) \qquad\qquad\qquad\qquad assignment$$

$$live(S_1; S_2; \ldots; S_n):$$
$$live(S_1) \quad \wedge \quad \bigwedge_{i=2}^{n} \square\,(at\ S_i \supset live(S_i)) \qquad\qquad composition$$

$$live(\text{if } B \text{ then } S_1 \text{ else } S_2 \text{ fi}):$$
$$(B \supset live(S_1)) \wedge (\sim B \supset live(S_2)) \qquad\qquad\qquad if$$

$$live(L: \quad \text{while } B \text{ do } S \text{ od}):$$
$$\square\big((at\ B \wedge B) \supset live(S)\big) \quad \wedge \qquad\qquad while$$
$$\big(\diamond(at\ B \wedge \sim B) \supset \diamond(after\ L)\big)$$

$$live(L: \quad \text{loop } S \text{ end loop}):$$
$$\square\diamond(live(S)) \wedge \square(\sim after\ L) \qquad\qquad\qquad\qquad loop$$

In the rules above, L is a statement label and S, $S1$, and $S2$ are statement lists. We assume that e and B contain no calls to monitor functions. Our scope rules then imply that the expressions e and B refer only to variables local to the process or monitor in question, and that evaluations of e and B are guaranteed to terminate. If necessary, any blockable functions can be computed separately, their values assigned to local temporary variables, and the temporary variables used in the actual expressions. This restriction simplifies our inference rules and is not an unreasonable requirement. An alternative approach would be to include the liveness criteria of the expression in the inference rules.

Figure 5.1–4

Live-assertions for Sequential VALET

5.1.5. *Commitments and Liveness Inference Rules*

The interpretation of at and *after* is the obvious one. If control is *after* S_1 in the statement list

$$S_1; S_2; S_3,$$

then it is at S_2. Similarly, control *after* the test in an **if** statement means that control is at one of the two branches; control *after* a branch means that control is *after* the **if**.

We now discuss the liveness properties of the rest of VALET. Monitor calls and **wait** statements can each be blocked in two different ways. As a result, they will require a stronger fairness rule than the other statements. As with sequential statements, monitor calls and **wait** statements can be delayed until their process is permitted to execute (obtains control of a processor). Our first liveness assumption guarantees that the statements will eventually be permitted to execute. However, these statements can also be blocked due to synchronization considerations. For example, **wait** statements can be blocked on their boolean condition, and monitor calls can be blocked trying to gain access to the monitor or on an internal wait of the monitor. To compound the problem, these two types of blocking, scheduling and synchronization, can interfere. Consider a process waiting on a boolean expression B inside a monitor. An adversary scheduler can make sure that the process was never scheduled when B was true. We therefore require that monitors be implemented in such a way that the following live-assertion for **wait** statements holds:

$$live(L:\ \ \text{wait}(B)):$$
$$\square\lozenge(MonitorFree \wedge B) \supset \lozenge(\text{after } L). \qquad \qquad \textit{wait}$$

The predicate *MonitorFree* is true when no module owns the monitor.

The final statement type is the monitor call. For each monitor procedure we specify, along with the pre- and post-assertions, a live-assertion. We derive the live-assertion of a monitor call as the composition of the live-assertions of the statements that comprise the body of the call. We must also formalize when *MonitorFree* is true. It is true when the monitor is released at a **wait** statement:

$$\text{at wait} \wedge R \quad \supset \quad \lozenge(MonitorFree \wedge R).$$

It is also true after the last statement of the procedure body:

$$\text{after } <body> \wedge R \quad \supset \quad \lozenge(MonitorFree \wedge R) \wedge \lozenge(\text{after } <call>).$$

For the purposes of verifying the liveness properties of the calling module, we shall only be interested in those liveness properties of the procedure that

5.1.5. Commitments and Liveness Inference Rules

are true when *MonitorFree* is true. Therefore, we restrict the live-assertions of a monitor call to statements concerning the initial conditions of the call, the termination of the call, and the predicates that are true when *MonitorFree* is true. We shall abbreviate the live-assertions of a monitor call by dropping the references to *MonitorFree*. For example, if we have proved for procedure X of monitor M that

$$\text{at } X \wedge P \wedge \square\Diamond(B \wedge M.\text{MonitorFree}) \quad \supset \quad \Diamond(R \wedge M.\text{MonitorFree}),$$

then the live assertion for $M.X$ would be written as

$$P \wedge \square\Diamond(B) \quad \supset \quad \Diamond(R).$$

Note the we have neglected exceptions, divide-by-zero errors, overflows, and the like. Formal rules for proving liveness properties including these problems, are a topic for further research.

There is one additional point about wait statements. In general, we require the boolean condition of a wait statement be true infinitely often in order to guarantee that the wait terminates. If, however, it can be shown that only the waiting process can cause the condition to become false, then (as long as the monitor is released infinitely often) requiring that the condition eventually becomes true suffices. The revised rule is

$$\text{live}(L: \quad \text{wait}(B)):$$
$$\Diamond(B \wedge \text{MonitorFree}) \wedge \square\Diamond(\text{MonitorFree}) \quad \supset \quad \Diamond(\text{after } L). \qquad \text{wait}'$$

▶**Proof of** *wait'*:

Let $B' = (B \wedge \text{MonitorFree})$. The original version of the wait live-assertion is

$$\square\Diamond(B') \quad \supset \quad \Diamond(\text{after } L). \tag{1}$$

Our assumption that only the waiting process can make B false can be written as

$$\text{at } L \wedge \Diamond(B') \wedge \square(\sim \text{after } L) \quad \supset \quad \Diamond\square(\text{MonitorFree} \supset B) \wedge \square\Diamond(\text{MonitorFree}). \tag{2}$$

Re-arranging (2) we obtain

$$\text{at } L \wedge \Diamond(B') \quad \supset \quad \Diamond(\text{after } L) \vee \square\Diamond(B'). \tag{3}$$

Therefore, assertions (1) and (3) imply

$$\text{at } L \wedge \Diamond(B') \quad \supset \quad \Diamond(\text{after } L),$$

which implies *wait'*. ■

5.1.6. Monitor and Process Specifications

There are three components of a monitor's specification: the invariants, the commitments, and the service specifications. Processes are specfied by invariants and commitments. This section describes these three types of specification assertions, and how to prove them from the code.

Monitors

Invariants describe the state of the monitor when no process is active within the monitor. For example, in a stack monitor we prove that the number of completed *pop* operations do not exceed the number of *push* operations. In a buffer monitor we prove that output from the buffer corresponds to input to the buffer. To prove that an assertion is a monitor invariant we show two properties: the initial condition implies the assertion, and the assertion is preserved over each monitor procedure. To show that the assertion is preserved, we prove that if the assertion is true at every point that the procedure gains control of the monitor (at the beginning or after a wait), then the assertion will be re-established before the procedure relinquishes control (at the end or at a wait).

Commitments are to liveness as invariants are to safety. Commitments state the properties that a monitor guarantees to make true. They include assertions that the state of the monitor will change, that output will be produced, and that buffers will not be always full or always empty. Commitments are proved by combining the liveness properties of the components of the monitor with assumptions about the environment of the monitor.

Finally, we must describe the services that the monitor provides to the calling environment. Service specifications consist of the pre-, post-, and live-assertions that are visible to the processes that call the monitor. As with sequential statements, if the pre-assertion is true before a monitor procedure is called and the procedure terminates, then the post-assertion will be true. We prove the relationship between a pre- and post-assertion by using the standard safety inference rules on the body of the procedure. In a similar way, we verify the live-assertion for a monitor service by using the liveness inference rules on the body of the procedure. Pre- and post-assertions will refer only to variables that are private to the calling process. This restriction allows use to conclude that if process X causes the pre-assertion P to become true before a call to the monitor, then no other process can invalidate P while X is waiting to gain control of the monitor. Similarly, if Q is true upon return from the monitor, it will still be true when X executes the next statement after the monitor call.

5.1.6. Monitor and Process Specifications

Live-assertions, on the other hand, can refer to non-private variables of the monitor. If a live-assertion states that eventually a buffer will be empty, then it will be empty when the monitor is released, but it may not be empty when the calling process begins to execute the next instruction after the monitor call.

The proofs in this thesis will vary in their formality. Many termination proofs will be informal; it will be obvious that there are no blockable statements in a section of code, or the conditions that could block a statement have been proved to be impossible. In other cases, the proofs will consist of detailed outlines as to how each statement in a procedure affects an invariant or commitment. All the proofs can be made rigorous.

We have restricted what internal information of a monitor is visible to the calling environment. Sometimes information about a monitor that is not necessary for the correct operation of the calling environment is needed for a proof in the calling environment. For example, the shared stack shown in Section 5.1.3 provided only *push* and *pop* as visible operations. A proof of a module using the shared-stack as a submodule might need information as to when *push* and *pop* operations terminate. A *push* terminates if the stack is not full and a *pop* terminates if the stack is not empty.

A proof of the calling module could be based upon the expressions $top = size$ and $top = 0$, but that would violate our visibility constraints. The solution to this dilemma is to allow modules to provide auxiliary *functions*, which are not implemented (as auxiliary variables are not implemented), but can be used in proofs. Auxiliary functions are visible to the calling module (or rather to the calling module's proof), but cannot affect the control flow of the calling module. We restrict auxiliary functions to returning a value, that is, auxiliary functions have no side effects. In our shared-stack example we could add the auxiliary functions *full* and *empty*:

auxiliary function *full* $\equiv$ *top=size*
auxiliary function *empty* $\equiv$ *top=0*

It is often convenient to make an internal variable visible to a proof of the external environment. In this case, we shall still use an auxiliary function, and we shall use the same name as the variable.

Processes

As with a monitors, we specify a processes with invariants and commitments. Processes, unlike monitors, provide no functions that can be called by other modules; hence, a process's specification does not include a service specification.

We can use loop invariants to prove properties of a process, but we specify a process's safety characteristics with general invariants, which must always be true. Such invariants are proved using standard verification techniques.

Commitments specify the liveness properties of a process and are derived from the combination of the live-assertions of the statements that constitute the process.

5.2. Heuristics

Suppose that we have a well-structured program that we want to verify. How do we go about it? It would be convenient to have a fixed set of rules that would always generate a proof, if one exists. That is beyond the scope of this thesis (and is, in general, difficult). However, this section gives some simple heuristics to help in constructing a proof. There is a significant bootstrapping problem in describing these heuristics. If the rules are given before the examples, then the rules are unmotivated and difficult to understand. If the examples are given before the rules, then the reader has no global overview of the verification process. Our compromise is to present a series of simple examples along with the heuristics.

Some of the heuristics, such as the first, are general. Others apply only in certain situations. Some heuristics contradict each other. This should not be too surprising because different approaches are needed for different problems.

Heuristic 1. *Hide the code as soon as possible.*

At the lowest level, the properties of processes and monitors are verified by examining their code. In constructing the module proof, we use the verified properties and can ignore the internal structure of the module implementations. For example, buffers are an abstract data type that can be implemented in many ways. Any implementation meeting the requirements of the data type can be used in a larger system without affecting the correctness proof of the rest of that system.

Unbounded Buffer

Our first example is an unbounded buffer. We wish to prove that the buffer faithfully transmits the data sent to it. We assume that there is an unbounded-array data type (that is, an array with an unbounded number of elements). The code for the buffer is shown in Figure 5.2–1. We assume that the buffer has one sender and one receiver.

> **Heuristic 2.** *Define input and output histories; relate the contents (or size) of one to that of the other.*

The safety property we wish to prove is that the output looks like the input. We therefore define input history α and output history β. The first is updated whenever something is stored in the buffer. The second is updated when something is removed. Our desired monitor invariant is

$$\beta \preceq \alpha. \tag{1}$$

The buffer includes the following two services.

send(m)

    pre: $\alpha = A$
    post: $\alpha = A < m >$

receive(var m)

    pre: $\beta = B$
    post: $\beta = B < m >$

Note that the specification above requires that there be exactly one sender and one receiver, because α and β must be private to the calling process to be included in the pre- or post-assertions.

> **Heuristic 3.** *Consider the program in isolation from its environment. There are often useful properties that can be proved immediately from the code, such as the termination of a simple procedure or the blocking conditions of a monitor call.*

We make no assumptions about what integers are stored, or even about the element-type of the array. This allows the proof to be used for a buffer containing any element type.

The code, with the addition of α and β, is presented in Figure 5.2–2. An auxiliary function *empty* has also been added for use later in the proof.

buffer: monitor

var
      buf: array [*1* .. ∞] of *integer*
      head, tail: *0* .. ∞

visible procedure *send* (*i*: *integer*)
begin
      head := *head* +*1*
      buf [*head*] := *i*
end procedure

visible procedure *receive* (**var** *i*: *integer*)
begin
      wait (*head* > *tail*)
      tail := *tail* + *1*
      return (*buf* [*tail*])
end procedure

begin
      head := *0*
      tail := *0*
end monitor

Figure 5.2–1
Unbounded Buffer

```
buffer: monitor
{ auxiliary variables added }
var
      buf: array [ 1 .. ∞ ] of integer
      head, tail: 0 .. ∞
      α, β: private history of integer

visible procedure send ( i: integer )
begin
      head := head + 1
      buf [ head ] := i
      α := α @ i
end procedure

visible procedure receive ( var i: integer )
begin
      wait ( head > tail )
      tail := tail + 1
      β := β @ buf [ tail ]
      return ( buf [ tail ] )
end procedure

auxiliary function empty ≡ ( head=tail )

begin
      head := 0
      tail := 0
      α := ∅
      β := ∅
end monitor
```

Note that @ is the history concatenation operator.

Figure 5.2-2
Unbounded Buffer with History Variables

5.2. Heuristics

> **Heuristic 4.** *Eliminate the role of local variables by relating them to visible functions or auxiliary variables. This will allow you to abstract from the details of the implementation and to make important information visible in the calling environment.*

▶**Proof of** (1):

We first prove three invariants, local to the monitor, that relate the contents of the histories to the contents of the array.

$$head \geq tail. \tag{2}$$

We prove (2) by showing that it is true initially:

$$head = tail = 0.$$

Then we demonstrate that each operation of the monitor preserves (2). It is obvious that *tail* can be incremented only when *head* is strictly greater than *tail*; hence, *head* will never be less than *tail*.

The second invariant relates α to *buf*:

$$\forall i \leq |\alpha|(\alpha_i = buf[i]) \quad \wedge \quad head = |\alpha|. \tag{3}$$

This is true initially because $|\alpha| = 0$. The only operation on α is *send*; it always stores the same information in *buf* as in α.

Similarly, the third invariant is

$$\forall i \leq |\beta|(\beta_i = buf[i]) \quad \wedge \quad tail = |\beta|. \tag{4}$$

This can be proved by showing that *tail* is never incremented without storing the corresponding element of *buf* into β, and by showing that nothing is stored into β without *tail* first being incremented.

By (2), (3) and (4) we derive

$$|\beta| \leq |\alpha| \quad \wedge \quad \forall i \leq |\beta|(\beta_i = buf[i] = \alpha_i)),$$

which implies (1). ∎

5.2. Heuristics

Invariant (1) would be satisfied by a buffer that never adds anything to β; in that case no output would ever appear. The promise that output will appear is a liveness commitment.

What liveness properties can we show about the buffer services without making assumptions about the buffer's environment? We can prove that *send* always terminates, because it has no internal wait statements. The *receive* operation, however, can block if *head* is less than or equal to *tail*. Assertion (2), however restricts this case to

$$head = tail,$$

which is the same as the auxiliary function *empty*. The live-statements for the buffer services are as follows.

send(m)

  live: $\Diamond(\text{after send})$

receive(var m)

  live: $\Box\Diamond(\sim empty) \supset \Diamond(\text{after receive})$

▶**Proof of** Live-assertions:

The live-assertion for *send* is true because *send* contains no wait statements. The live-assertion for *receive* is a conjunction of the live-assertions for the statements of *receive*—the only possibility of blocking comes from the wait statement on *empty*. ▯

If we are willing to assume that there is only one receiving process, then the last live statement can be transformed to

$$\Diamond(\sim empty) \supset \Diamond(\text{after receive}),$$

because then only the single receiver can make a non-empty buffer empty.

This is as far as we can go without making assumptions about the environment of the buffer. Rather than extend this example, we shall discuss a bounded buffer and extend that example to an entire system.

5.2. Heuristics

Bounded Buffer

Our next example is a system of five modules: a sender, a receiver, a bounded buffer (the same as an unbounded buffer, except that it can be filled), a source of data, and a sink for data.

> **Heuristic 5.** *Reason about unbounded sequences of operations.*

We shall assume that $\overline{X}$, our source of data, is unbounded: it will keep producing data as often as it is asked. We also assume that the sink $\overline{Y}$ is unbounded, so it can accept data as often as data is sent. The sender will read data from $\overline{X}$ and send it to the buffer. The receiver will read data from the buffer and send it to $\overline{Y}$. The diagram of the system is in Figure 5.2–3 and the code for the sender and the receiver is shown in Figure 5.2–4. Note that we include the history variables in the system diagram. They are located next to their monitor and on the data path they record.

The histories of the system are X, Y, α, and β. The *read* operation reads data from the source, and the *write* operation sends data to the sink. We assume that both *read* and *write* always terminate.

The bounded buffer that is used in this system is not defined by program code; it is essentially a black box about which we have limited information. What we know about the buffer are its specifications, and these might be verified by examining the code of lower-level components of the system, just as the specifications of the unbounded buffer were verified from its code.

The specifications of the buffer consist of two invariants, two services (*send* and *receive*), and two auxiliary functions (*empty* and *full*). The first invariant states that data comes out of the buffer in the same order that data went in to the buffer:

$$\beta \preceq \alpha. \tag{1}$$

The second invariant relates the value of *empty* to that of *full*:

$$empty \supset \sim full. \tag{2}$$

The service specifications follow. The live-assertions require that there is exactly one sender and one receiver.

send(i)

    pre: $\alpha = A$
    post: $\alpha = A < i >$
    live: $\Diamond(\sim full) \supset \Diamond(after\ send) \wedge \Diamond(\sim empty)$

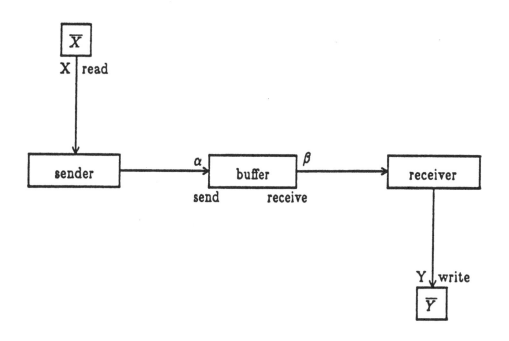

Figure 5.2–3
Bounded Buffer System

```
sender: process
var
      i: integer
      X, α: private history of integer
begin
      loop
            X̄.read(i)
            buffer.send(i)
      end loop
end process


receiver: process
var
      j: integer
      Y, β: private history of integer
begin
      loop
            buffer.receive(j)
            Ȳ.write(j)
      end loop
end process
```

Figure 5.2–4
Bounded Buffer

5.2. *Heuristics*

receive(var i)

    pre: $\beta = B$
    post: $\beta = B < i >$
    live: $\Diamond(\sim empty) \supset \Diamond(after\ receive) \wedge \Diamond(\sim full)$

We want to show that the output history looks like the input history:

$$Y \preceq X. \tag{3}$$

As in the unbounded-buffer example, assertion (3) does not guarantee that any output is produced. For that we need a liveness commitment:

$$u(Y). \tag{4}$$

That is, the length of Y grows without bound.

In order to prove assertions (3) and (4), we must state and prove the invariants and commitments for the sender and the receiver.

▶**Proof of** (3):

It is simple to prove the following invariants. The first invariant describes the sender; the second describes the receiver:

$$\alpha \preceq X \tag{5}$$

$$Y \preceq \beta. \tag{6}$$

Assertions (1), (5), and (6) immediately imply (3).   ■

▶**Proof of** (4):

Because we are assuming that *read* and *write* do not block, the commitments of the sender (7) and receiver (8) are also simple:

$$\Box\Diamond(\sim buffer.full) \supset \Box\Diamond(\sim buffer.empty) \tag{7}$$

$$\Box\Diamond(\sim buffer.empty) \supset u(Y). \tag{8}$$

These two commitments are a consequence of the **loop** (liveness) inference rule and the service specifications of the buffer. The inference rule, as applied to the *sender*, states that

$$\Box\Diamond(live(read;\ send)).$$

5.2. *Heuristics*

Because *read* operations always terminate,

$$\Box\Diamond(live(read;send))$$

becomes

$$\Box\Diamond(live(send)),$$

or by substituting the live-assertion for *send*,

$$\Box\Diamond(\Diamond(\sim buffer.full) \supset \Diamond(after\ send) \wedge \Diamond(\sim buffer.empty)).$$

This formula implies

$$\Box\Diamond(\sim buffer.full) \supset \Box\Diamond(\sim buffer.empty),$$

which is (7). The proof of (8) is similar, involving the pre- and post-assertions of *receive*.

> **Heuristic 6.** *Prove the absence of deadlock early—it will simplify the liveness hypotheses.*

The conclusions of (7) and (8) are true if the buffer does not become permanently full or permanently empty. Such a situation would imply that deadlock has occurred, because one process must be stuck, not doing the appropriate *send* or *receive*. To eliminate the possibility of deadlock, we need to show that

$$\Box\Diamond(\sim buffer.empty).$$

First we examine (7); it can be rearranged to yield

$$\Diamond\Box(buffer.full) \vee \Box\Diamond(\sim buffer.empty). \tag{7'}$$

We can restate (2) as

$$\Diamond\Box(buffer.full) \supset \Diamond\Box(\sim buffer.empty). \tag{2'}$$

Because $\Diamond\Box P \supset \Box\Diamond P$ we conclude, using 2' and 7', that

$$\Box\Diamond(\sim buffer.empty),$$

which satisfies the hypothesis of (8). Therefore, the conclusion of (8), which is $u(Y)$, is true. ∎

5.2. Heuristics

Semaphores

The last example in this chapter is contrived, but it is useful for introducing four more heuristics that will be useful in Chapters 6 and 7. The example is an implementation of semaphores (to be used for mutual exclusion) using monitors. We define a semaphore that is to be shared among several users. The semaphore will insure that critical sections are executed in mutual exclusion. The code for the example is in Figure 5.2-5.

We assume that when a process wishes to enter a critical section, it does a P operation on a mutex semaphore. When the critical section is exited, the user performs a V operation. Critical sections are assumed to have no blockable code. We wish to show that mutual exclusion is enforced and that every process wishing to enter its critical section will eventually be able to do so.

In Figure 5.2-5, *sem* initially has the value 1. P operations wait until *sem* is positive and then decrement *sem* to indicate that there is a process in its critical section. V operations unconditionally increment *sem*.

The desired safety property is that no two processes be within their critical sections at the same time.

> **Heuristic 7.** *Abstract information from the histories to suppress irrelevant details. For example, relate the monitor state to the size of its histories.*

> **Heuristic 8.** *Maintain histories of each process.*

To state this safety property we must determine how many users are within a critical section. We accomplish this by recording the Ps and Vs of each process in a private variable. This information can be recorded in two ways: a history of the form $PVPV\ldots$, or a count of the number of Ps minus the number of Vs that the process has executed. We choose the latter because it is simpler. We add a private variable, *changes*, to record the difference. The desired safety property becomes

$$\forall i(changes[i] = 0) \lor \exists! i\, (changes[i] = 1 \land \forall j \neq i\, (changes[j] = 0)).$$

The notation $\exists! i$ means "there exists a unique i."

To hide the exact implementation of the semaphore, we add an auxiliary function *free* to indicate when a process can proceed. The modified code is shown in Figure 5.2-6. Remember that the auxiliary variable **id** represents the indentifier of the calling process.

```
mutex: monitor
constant
      num=1 { number of process allowed in critical
                  section at the same time }
var
      sem: integer

visible procedure P
begin
      wait (sem>0)
      sem := sem - 1
end procedure

visible procedure V
begin
      sem := sem + 1
end procedure

begin
      sem := num
end monitor
```

Figure 5.2–5
Semaphores

```
mutex: monitor
{with auxiliary variables}
constant
        num=1 {number of process allowed in critical
                      section at the same time}
var
        sem: integer
        changes: private integer {one per calling process}

visible procedure P
begin
        wait (sem>0)
        sem := sem - 1
        changes [id]  := changes [id] + 1
end procedure

visible procedure V
begin
        sem := sem + 1
        changes [id]  := changes [id] - 1
end procedure

auxiliary function free ≡ (sem>0)

begin
        sem := num
        ∀ i (changes [i] := 0)
end monitor
```

Figure 5.2–6

Semaphores with Auxiliary Variables

5.2. Heuristics

We relate *sem* to the sum of the *changes* elements:

$$sem = 1 - \sum_i changes[i]. \tag{1}$$

This is an invariant local to the monitor, because *sem* is not visible from the outside. The proof of (1) is simple because it is true initially, and *sem* is only decremented when a *changes* element is incremented, and vice versa.

If we were to look at the monitor in isolation, there would be many possible effects of mixing *P* and *V* operations in an arbitrary manner. To state all such possibilities would take a long time and would serve no purpose; our knowledge about the calling processes rules out many of these cases.

Heuristic 9. *Consider the module in context.*

We note here that Heuristic 9 contradicts Heuristic 3. There are many simple properties that can be proved directly from the code of a module (for example, showing that a monitor call with no blockable statements is guaranteed to terminate). More complicated properties that depend on the order that procedures are called or the values passed in the parameter list can be more easily stated if the "correct" operation of the calling environment is taken as a hypothesis.

Our statement of the problem implies that the calling processes will execute *P* and *V* operations in the correct order; we state this assumption as

$$(i \text{ at } P \supset changes[i] = 0) \quad \wedge \quad (i \text{ at } V \supset changes[i] = 1). \tag{I}$$

This assumption would have to be verified in a higher-level proof in which the calling processes are considered. The remaining two monitor invariants are

$$I \quad \supset \quad \forall i(0 \leq changes[i] \leq 1) \tag{2}$$

and

$$I \quad \supset \quad (\sim free \supset \exists!i(changes[i] = 1)) \\ \wedge \quad (free \supset \forall i(changes[i] = 0)) \tag{3}$$

Outlines of the proofs of invariants (2) and (3) are shown in Figures 5.2-7 and 5.2-8. The three invariants imply the desired mutual exclusion invariant.

The service safety specifications are as follows:

Proof of

$$I \quad \supset \quad \forall i (0 \le changes[i] \le 1) \tag{2}$$

Initially:
    $\forall i (changes[i] := 0)$
    $\{(2)\}$

$\{I \wedge (2)\}$
visible procedure P
begin
    $\{changes[id] = 0 \wedge (2)\}$
    wait $(sem > 0)$
    $\{changes[id] = 0 \wedge (2)\}$
    $\ldots$
    $changes[id] := changes[id] + 1$
    $\{changes[id] = 1 \wedge (2)\}$
end procedure
$\{(2)\}$

$\{I \wedge (2)\}$
visible procedure V
begin
    $\{changes[id] = 1\}$
    $\ldots$
    $changes[id] := changes[id] - 1$
    $\{changes[id] = 0\}$
end procedure
$\{(2)\}$

Figure 5.2-7
Proof of Invariant 2

Proof of

$$I \quad \supset \quad (\sim free \supset \exists !i(changes[i] = 1))$$
$$\wedge \quad (free \supset \forall i(changes[i] = 0))$$

(3)

Initially:
    sem := *1*
    { *free* }
    $\forall i$ (*changes* [*i*] := *0*)
    { (3) }

{ *I* $\wedge$ (2) $\wedge$ (3) }
visible procedure *P*
begin
    { *changes* [id] =*0* }
    wait (*sem>0*)
    { (2) $\wedge$ (3) $\wedge$ *changes* [id] =*0* $\wedge$ *free* }
    { *therefore:* $\forall i$ (*changes* [*i*] =*0*) }
    sem := *sem* - *1*
    { $\forall i$ (*changes* [*i*] =*0*) $\wedge \sim$ *free* }
    changes [id] := *changes* [id] + *1*
    { $\exists !i$ (*changes* [*i*] =*1*) $\wedge \sim$ *free* }
end procedure
{ (3) }

{ *I* $\wedge$ (1) $\wedge$ (2) $\wedge$ (3) }
visible procedure *V*
begin
    { *changes* [id] =*1* $\wedge$ (1) $\wedge$ (2) $\wedge$ (3) }
    { *therefore:* $\sim$ *Free* }
    { *therefore:* $\forall i{\neq}$id (*changes* [*i*] =*0*) }
    { *therefore:* *sem* $=$ 0 }
    sem := *sem* + *1*
    { *free* $\wedge$ *changes* [id] =*1* $\wedge$ $\forall i{\neq}$id (*changes* [*i*] =*0*) }
    changes [id] := *changes* [id] - *1*
    { *free* $\wedge$ $\forall i$ (*changes* [*i*] =*0*) }
end procedure
{ (3) }

Figure 5.2–8
Proof of Invariant 3

5.2. Heuristics

P

    pre: $changes[id] = 0$
    post: $changes[id] = 1$

V

    pre: $changes[id] = 1$
    post: $changes[id] = 0.$

The liveness specifications of P and V follow; they are derived directly from the code.

P

    live: $\Box\Diamond free \supset \Diamond(after\ P) \land \Diamond(free)$

V

    live: $\Diamond(after\ V)$

The liveness property that we wish to prove is that calls to P and V always terminate (under the current assumptions).

Heuristic 10.   *Reason about single operations.*

In Heuristic 5, we suggested reasoning about unbounded sequences of operations. Such reasoning is useful for proving general properties of communication media and buffers that are anticipated to handle a large number of messages. On the other hand, if we are proving the properties of a monitor call, we do not want the call's effect to be dependent on subsequent operations. In these circumstances, we reason about the properties of single operations.

The V operation obviously terminates, because it contains no wait statements or internal monitor calls. The P operation is more complex. Using the context of the system, we assume that if a process issues a P, then it will eventually finish its critical section and issue a V. The temporal statement of this system commitment is

$$\forall i \Box(changes[i] = 1 \supset \Diamond(changes[i] = 0)). \qquad (C)$$

Our desired monitor commitment then becomes

$$C \quad \supset \quad \Box\Diamond free. \qquad (4)$$

If we can prove (4), then we have shown that the P operation will terminate unconditionally.

Chapter 6
Network Protocols

Programs that implement computer communication protocols can exhibit extremely complicated behavior, because they must cope with asynchronous computing agents and with the possibility of failures in both the agents and the communication medium. Most previous approaches to verifying network protocols have been based upon reachability arguments for finite-state models of the protocols. However, only protocols of limited complexity can be verified using finite-state models, because of the combinatorial explosion of the state space as the complexity of the protocol increases. Finite-state models also have difficulty in expressing properties related to correct data transfer. In contrast, the approach described here models a protocol as a parallel program, and correctness proofs follow the Floyd/Hoare style of program verification. Logical assertions attached to the program abstract information from the representation of the state to allow reasoning about classes of states. This avoids the combinatorial explosion, and the length of the proof need not grow unmanageably as the protocol size increases.

The first two sections of this chapter describe network protocols and the techniques that have been used to verify them. The remaining five sections present protocols from the literature and proofs of the correctness of these protocols.

6.1. Introduction

This section provides an introduction to network protocols. The next section presents a history of protocol verification. The major sources for the information in this introduction are Stenning [44], McQuillan, and Cerf [30].

We model the network/protocol system as a set of interacting modules that represent logical units of the system, such as the communication medium, transmitter, and receiver. The processes (or nodes of the network) can be implemented with one process per processor, or they can be multiprogrammed on a single processor. The media can be implemented by physical wires, FIFO queues, synchronized channels, or more complicated modules that incorporate processes and monitors.

Stenning defines a protocol in the context of computer networks as "a set of rules designed to enable interaction between two or more communicating parties." A protocol is defined by McQuillan and Cerf as a logical specification

5.2. Heuristics

▶**Proof of** (4):

We prove (4) by contradiction. Suppose that

$$C \quad \wedge \quad \diamond\square(\sim free).$$

This assumption coupled with invariant (3) implies

$$C \quad \wedge \quad \diamond\square(\exists! i(changes[i] = 1)). \tag{5}$$

In other words, eventually some process will have a value of *changes* equal to 1, while all other process have *changes* equal to 0. Formula (5) does not imply that the same process always has *changes* = 1, but rather that there is always some process that does. Commitment C rules out the possibility that one process can always have *changes* = 1, because C states that *changes* will eventually become 0. In this implementation, however, it is impossible for the value of *changes* for two different processes to change during one monitor call, because *changes* is private to the calling process. Therefore, we can prove that

$$\exists! i \, (changes[i] = 1) \quad \supset \quad \diamond(\forall i \, (changes[i] = 0)),$$

which contradicts the assumption. ∎

Conclusion

There is one remaining heuristic, which is not used until Chapter 7; it will be discussed there.

Heuristic 11. *Make virtual data structures explicit.*

6.1. Introduction

of the communication process, specifying three aspects of the communication: a standard data element, a set of transmission conventions, and a description of the standard communication paths. The specification of a protocol also includes the set of primitive operations and data types that the protocol has available from the system on which it is implemented, and the set of services that the protocol must provide to the users of the network.

The specification of a standard data element depends on which primitive operations are available. If the primitive operations include changing the voltage on a physical wire, then the standard data element may be a bit; the protocol specifies what a *zero* and *one* look like. A higher level protocol can define characters in terms of bits, packets in terms of characters, or variable-length files in terms of fixed-length packets. A protocol, however, need not provide a data element different from the primitive data element it uses. For example, a protocol can provide a reliable virtual channel for messages built on an unreliable physical channel for the same class of messages.

The hallmark of a protocol is the service it provides and how it provides that service. Transmission conventions represent the "how." Such conventions specify when messages should be sent, how long the sender should wait before assuming a message has been lost, when the receiver should send an acknowledgment, and so on. For example, in providing a reliable service on an unreliable medium, the conventions would specify the rules for using sequence numbers, timers, and acknowledgments. Transmission conventions also specify the control information format and the message format.

The specification of the standard communication path provides an address structure so that each process can refer to other processes in the network. The path structure can also specify traffic control, error correction, priority schemes, and the rules for initiating and terminating conversations.

Communication paths can be implemented as direct links between each each pair of processes in the network. This approach becomes uneconomical as the number of nodes in the network increases. Depending on how the network is used, it may be possible to share communication paths. A protocol would then provide a virtual, fully-connected network on a physical network with shared communication lines. Two mechanisms in current use for sharing communication links are *circuit switching* and *packet switching*. An example of a circuit switching network is the telephone system. The circuits are shared resources that are allocated and de-allocated as needed. Once a circuit is allocated to a pair of processes, it becomes dedicated to that conversation until it is no longer needed. Packet switching networks multiplex the shared links between more than one conversation by sending data in packets; each packet is identified by the names of the sender and the intended receiver.

6.2. Verification

One communication line can be used by many conversations at the same time, and one conversation can use more than one physical link. The packets can be stored at intermediate network nodes, routed around "traffic jams," and otherwise handled by many processes until they are finally delivered. This thesis will only be concerned with protocols for packet switching networks.

The services that a network provides can be specified either by a single-level protocol or by a hierarchy of protocols. Hierarchical design allows for a separation between the different functions of a protocol. This simplifies the specification, the design, and the implementation of the network. For the purpose of verification, such structured design allows levels to be verified separately, reducing the complexity of the proofs.

6.2. Verification

This section discusses formal techniques that have been used to verify network protocols; it is based on the works of Stenning [44] and Sunshine [45].

Formal techniques for verifying protocols fall into three categories: finite-state models, parallel-program models, and unified models. Finite-state models describe a protocol as a set of finite-state machines (or similar machines such as Petri nets, colloquies, or regular expressions). Liveness proofs of finite-state models involve reachability analysis on the set of possible state configurations. Parallel-program models describe the protocol as a parallel program and use standard program-verification tools to prove desired properties. The unified approach is a combination of the first two, in which states in the finite-state machine have variables associated with them to abstract information from the bare machine.

The finite-state approach covers the basic operation of a protocol: message input, message output, and timeout. Each process in the protocol is represented by a finite-state machine (for example, one each for a reader, a writer, and a communication medium). Every possible state of each process is represented by a state in the finite-state machine for that process. The states within a machine are linked by transitions that represent some external event, such as receipt of a message. A finite-state machine for the alternating bit protocol [1] is shown in Figure 6.2–1. The alternating bit protocol is discussed in Section 6.4.

The state of a protocol is an n-tuple of machine states; the state of each of the n finite-state machines in the protocol represents one element of the n-tuple. Reachability analysis determines which of these system states can be encountered during execution of the system. System states with no transitions

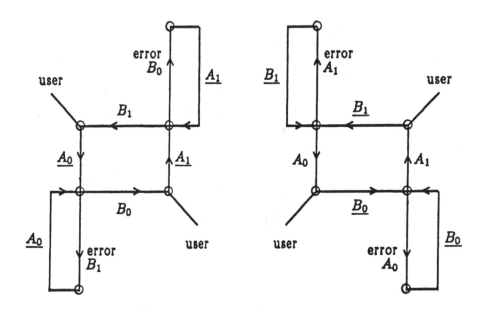

Process A   Process B

The transmission or receipt of a message is represented by a transition. Transmissions are underlined. The subscripts represent the sequence number of the message (0 or 1). Diagonal lines indicate input from or output to an external user.

Figure 6.2–1
The Alternating Bit Protocol

leaving them represent deadlock. A comprehensive reachability analysis can determine if such deadlocked states are possible and under what circumstances they might be encountered.

The main advantage of the finite-state model is that the generation of system states (as combinations of the individual machine states) and the reachability analysis can be automated [41, 47, 48]. The main disadvantage is that only protocols of a limited size can be verified using this technique. As the complexity of the protocol increases, there is a combinatorial explosion in the size of the system state space. State space reduction techniques have been used to help reduce the explosion. Eventually, however, the exponential growth makes the proofs unmanageable. Another shortcoming of finite-state models is that they do not address the important area of data definition: the correctness of the message contents and the order in which these messages are received.

Parallel-program models treat a protocol as a system of concurrent processes. Stenning [43, 44] specifies and verifies a data transfer protocol and a connection control protocol using standard assertions and non-interference techniques [32, 33]. The verification involves only safety properties of the protocols. More recently Bremer and Drobnik [5] have attempted to exploit modularization in their safety proofs. This thesis presents a technique for proving both safety and liveness properties of protocols.

Bochmann [3] has developed the unified method, which combines the finite-state and the parallel-program models. A set of finite-state machines represent the control structure of the protocol. The semantic structure (for example, the values of sequence numbers) is represented by variables attached to the states and by enabling predicates on the transitions. This combination allows the reachability analysis to detect deadlock errors while permitting logical statements about the data definition. The additional semantic information can affect the control flow. Because the control flow can be affected by the semantic information, reachability analysis alone does not suffice to detect all deadlock situations. On the other hand, some data definition properties can be proved using assertional techniques.

6.3. The Communication Medium

In this chapter, the communication media are not defined by program code; each medium is a black box about which we have limited information. What we know about the medium are its specifications. These specifications might be verified by examining the code of lower level components of the system, just as the specifications of the transmitters and receivers in the next few sections

6.3. The Communication Medium

will be verified from their code. Because of our hierarchical view of programs, we view each layer of a program as using a lower level of black boxes, and each level provides a new black box for the next higher program layer.

The medium specification, like the specification of a monitor, involves three kinds of information. First, there is an *invariant*: an assertion about the medium that is true at all times in the computation. The invariant describes the safety properties of the medium. Second, liveness properties are specified by temporal logic assertions called *commitments*. Commitments describe conditions that the medium causes to become true. Finally, the services provided by the medium (sending and receiving a message, checking for the presence of messages) must be precisely defined.

Possible models for a communication medium include synchronized communication [19], bounded buffer, unbounded buffer, and various kinds of unreliable transmissions lines. An unreliable transmission line can do one or more bad things to a message, such as lose, corrupt, duplicate, or re-order it. This section discusses an unreliable medium.

Consider a medium that can duplicate, lose, and re-order messages. We shall use this medium in Sections 6.5 and 6.6. The medium has input history α and output history β. Such a communication medium, being unreliable, has a weak invariant: nothing comes out that was not put in. This property is stated more precisely as

$$m \in \beta \quad \supset \quad m \in \alpha, \tag{1}$$

where m is any message. Invariant (1) implies that the medium neither creates spurious messages, nor corrupts existing messages.

The first invariant would be satisfied by a medium that never delivered any messages, and in that case no output would ever appear. We add two commitments that guarantee that some messages ultimately get through. The first is an assertion that if an unbounded number of messages are sent, then messages are infinitely often available to be received. It is stated as

$$u(\alpha) \quad \supset \quad \Box\Diamond(ExistsM), \tag{2}$$

where $ExistsM$ is a function of the medium that is true if a message is available to be received.

The second commitment asserts that if the same message is sent over and over again, it will eventually be delivered, provided that the receiving process keeps accepting messages. This is expressed by the formula

$$uc(\alpha, m) \wedge u(\beta) \quad \supset \quad \Diamond(m \in \beta). \tag{3}$$

6.3. The Communication Medium

The functions u and uc were defined in Section 5.1.3. The formula $u(\alpha)$ means that the length of history α grows without bound; the formula $uc(\alpha, m)$ indicates that message m will appear in history α an unbounded number of times.

To specify precisely the services of the medium we give pre-, post-, and live-assertions about each operation. The medium provides three services: send a message, receive a message, and check to see whether any messages are waiting to be received. We assume that the medium serves exactly one sender and one receiver.

send(m)

    pre: $\alpha = A$
    post: $\alpha = A < m >$
    live: $\Diamond(\text{after send})$

receive(var m)

    pre: $\beta = B$
    post: $\beta = B < m >$
    live: $\Diamond(ExistsM) \quad \supset \quad \Diamond(\text{after receive})$

ExistsM

    pre: $true$
    post: $true$
    live: $\Diamond(\text{after } ExistsM)$

Note that a *send* operation always terminates, and *receive* terminates if a message is available. The pre- and post-conditions of *ExistsM* are both true, which gives no safety information about the operation. The *ExistsM* function is not involved in the safe operation of a protocol. It is used only to guarantee that the *receive* operation will terminate (a liveness property).

The live-assertion for *receive* contains a hidden assumption about the operation of *ExistsM*. Our intuitive definition of *ExistsM* said that the function is true if there is a message to be received. Because we are assuming that there is only one receiver, if *ExistsM* becomes true, then it will not become false before a *receive* operation takes place. The additional monitor invariant that describes this property is

$$ExistsM \wedge \Box(\sim B \text{ after receive}) \quad \supset \quad \Box(ExistsM).$$

6.4. The Alternating Bit Protocol

In the field of network protocols, the alternating bit protocol is a classic. It was first published by Bartlett, Scantlebury, and Wilkinson [1] in 1969 in response to a paper by Lynch [27]. Lynch claimed that at least two control bits were necessary to send messages over transmission lines that cause errors. (Here, the term "error" implies that the communication medium can corrupt the contents of a message.) The alternating bit protocol, as shown in the finite-state machine of Figure 6.2–1, requires only one bit of control information to guarantee reliability.

The original protocol consists of two processes and a communication medium; both processes can send and receive data from outside users. We take a slightly different view of the protocol by restricting the services that the two processes provide and by including a second medium. Only process A will receive data from users, and only process B will send data to users. These changes to do not significantly change the problem, but they make the proof easier to understand. Process A reads data from an external unbounded source of data $\overline{X}$. The history of the data that the process has read is called X. A sequence bit and a datum are combined into a message, which is sent to process B by way of communication medium mab. Process B receives messages from mab, strips off the sequence bit, and outputs the data to the unbounded sink $\overline{Y}$. The history of the data that the process has output is denoted Y. Acknowledgments, consisting of a sequence bit and the datum "ack," are sent back to process A by way of medium mba. The histories α, β, γ, and δ record the messages sent to and from the media. Figure 6.4–1 shows the system diagram. The media are modeled as single-element buffers that can change a sequence number to the constant "error." Such a change represents a corruption of the datum. (This model of corruption is reasonable if we assume the existence of a lower-level mechanism that detects corrupted messages by using a checksum. The corrupted messages can be reported in the manner described above.) Our goal is to show that the protocol delivers the messages sent it in the correct order, in spite of the possibility of corruption by the medium. The code for processes A and B is presented in Figures 6.4–2 and 6.4–3.

The Communication Medium

Each medium is a single-element buffer (with the ability to corrupt messages). Because there is only one slot in the buffer, the auxiliary functions *full* and *empty* are opposites:

$$mab.empty \equiv \sim mab.full \qquad (mab1)$$

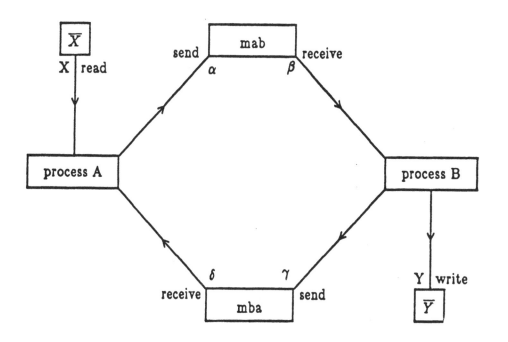

Figure 6.4–1
System Diagram for the Alternating Bit Protocol.

```
A: process
var
        WaitingForAck, Last Sent: integer { modulus = 2}
        data, ack: item
        ackno: (0, 1, error)
        α, δ, X: private history
begin
        { initialize}
        WaitingForAck := 1
        LastSent := 0

        loop
                { has the current message been acknowledged?}
                if LastSent ≠ WaitingForAck then
                        {read in new data}
                        LastSent := LastSent ⊕ 1
                        data := X̄.read
                fi

                {send new message}
                mab.send(LastSent, data)

                {wait for acknowledgment}
                mba.receive(ackno, ack)

                { is this an acknowledgment for the current message?}
                if ackno = WaitingForAck then
                        WaitingForAck := WaitingForAck ⊕ 1
                fi
        end loop
end process
```

Figure 6.4–2
Alternating Bit Protocol: Process A

```
B: process
var
      NextRequired: integer { modulus = 2 }
      messno: ( 0, 1, error )
      info: item
      β, γ, Y: private history
begin
      { initialize }
      NextRequired := 1

      loop
            { wait for next message }
            mab.receive( messno, info )

            { is this a new message? }
            if messno = NextRequired then
                  { process new message }
                  Ȳ.write( info )
                  NextRequired := NextRequired ⊕ 1
            fi

            { send acknowledgment }
            mba.send( NextRequired ⊖ 1, "ack" )
      end loop
end process
```

Figure 6.4-3
Alternating Bit Protocol: Process B

6.4. The Alternating Bit Protocol

$$mba.empty \equiv \sim mba.full. \qquad (mba1)$$

The second invariant asserts that the medium creates no new messages, loses no messages, and maintains the relative order of correct messages. We define the predicate $corrupted(m)$ to be true if the sequence bit of message m is error. Then the second invariant is

$$\beta_i = \alpha_i \quad \vee \quad corrupted(\beta_i) \qquad (mab2)$$

$$\delta_i = \gamma_i \quad \vee \quad corrupted(\delta_i), \qquad (mba2)$$

where α_k is the kth element of the history α. The third invariant relates the sizes of the histories to the state of the medium:

$$\text{if } mab.empty \text{ then } |\alpha| = |\beta| \text{ else } |\alpha| = |\beta| + 1 \qquad (mab3)$$

$$\text{if } mba.empty \text{ then } |\gamma| = |\delta| \text{ else } |\gamma| = |\delta| + 1. \qquad (mba3)$$

Each medium has one commitment. If message m is sent an unbounded number of times (and an unbounded number of receives are performed), then message m is received correctly an unbounded number of times. The commitment is stated as

$$uc(\alpha, m) \wedge u(\beta) \quad \supset \quad uc(\beta, m) \qquad (mab4)$$

$$uc(\gamma, m) \wedge u(\delta) \quad \supset \quad uc(\delta, m). \qquad (mba4)$$

Each medium provides two services, send and receive, and two auxiliary functions, empty and full. The services for mab are shown below. The services for mba are similar.

send(m)

```
pre:    α = A
post:   α = A < m >
live:   ◊(mab.empty)   ⊃   ◊(after mab.send)
```

receive(var m)

    pre: $\beta = B$
    post: $\beta = B < m >$
    live: $\Diamond(mab.full) \quad \supset \quad \Diamond(after\ mab.receive)$

The service specifications are based on the assumption that there is only one sender and one receiver for each medium. In Section 6.3 we required an additional invariant to describe the correct operation of *ExistsM*, here we constrain *full* and *empty* in a similar way. If a medium becomes full and no *receive* operations are executed on that medium, the medium remains full. Similarly, if a medium becomes empty and no *send* operations are executed on that medium, the medium remains empty. These constraints are stated formally as

$$mab.full \wedge \Box(\sim B\ after\ mab.receive) \quad \supset \quad \Box(mab.full)$$
$$mba.full \wedge \Box(\sim A\ after\ mba.receive) \quad \supset \quad \Box(mba.full)$$
$$mab.empty \wedge \Box(\sim A\ after\ mab.send) \quad \supset \quad \Box(mab.empty)$$
$$mba.empty \wedge \Box(\sim B\ after\ mba.send) \quad \supset \quad \Box(mba.empty).$$

The system liveness proof requires two more invariants for each medium. These invariants describe the length of the histories if one process becomes blocked:

$$A\ at\ mab.send \wedge \alpha = a \wedge \Box(\sim mab.empty) \quad \supset \quad \Box(\alpha = a) \quad (mab5)$$
$$B\ at\ mab.receive \wedge \beta = b \wedge \Box(\sim mab.full) \quad \supset \quad \Box(\beta = b) \quad (mab6)$$
$$B\ at\ mba.send \wedge \gamma = c \wedge \Box(\sim mba.empty) \quad \supset \quad \Box(\gamma = c) \quad (mba5)$$
$$A\ at\ mba.receive \wedge \delta = d \wedge \Box(\sim mba.full) \quad \supset \quad \Box(\delta = d) \quad (mba6)$$

Safety: Process A

The messages in history α are pairs, consisting of a sequence bit and a datum. We define the abbreviation M_i to be the contents of the message for the ith datum:

$$M_i = [i\ mod\ 2, X_i].$$

The first invariant of process A relates the histories X to α. (The history notation used in this section was defined in Section 5.1.3.) The invariant is

6.4. The Alternating Bit Protocol

stated as

$$\exists n \left(|X| = n \quad \wedge \quad \alpha = < M_i^+ >_{i=1}^{n-1} < M_n^* > \right). \qquad (A1)$$

In other words, when n items have been input to process A, the output to the mab medium is a sequence of repeated messages: one or more copies of M_1, then one or more copies of M_2, and so on, ending with zero or more copies of M_n. The last term is M_n^*, rather than M_n^+, because after the operation X.read, the nth piece of data has been read in, but message M_n has not yet been sent out. Figure 6.4-4 gives an outline of the proof of A1.

Each message of α contains a single bit for sequencing information. The full sequence number of a message is implied by examining the bit fields of the preceding messages in the history. A change in parity between successive elements signals a change in sequence numbers. We define $\#(\alpha, i)$ to be the number of changes in parity in α up to and including element i. The formal definition is

$$\#(\alpha, 0) = 0$$
$$\#(\alpha, 1) = 0 \qquad\qquad \text{if } \alpha_1.bit = 0$$
$$\#(\alpha, 1) = 1 \qquad\qquad \text{if } \alpha_1.bit = 1$$
$$\#(\alpha, i) = \#(\alpha, i-1) \qquad \text{if } i > 1 \wedge \alpha_i.bit = \alpha_{i-1}.bit$$
$$\#(\alpha, i) = \#(\alpha, i-1) + 1 \qquad \text{if } i > 1 \wedge \alpha_i.bit \neq \alpha_{i-1}.bit.$$

Note that the case $\#(\alpha, 1) = 0$ is impossible, in this system, because A1 states that if $|\alpha| \geq 1$, then $\alpha_1.bit = 1$.

The messages of δ are acknowledgments (and errors) of the form

$$[bit, \text{"ack"}],$$

where bit is an element of $\{0, 1, error\}$.

The second invariant of process A relates the sizes of α to δ:

$$|\delta| \leq |\alpha| \leq |\delta| + 1. \qquad (A2)$$

Relating the size of the two histories does not suffice to prove properties about the sequence numbers of the two histories. In order to state such properties we must define $\#$ on δ. The definition of $\#$ on α is not appropriate, because δ can contain errors, which are not included in the definition. Our solution is to create a new history that is equal to δ with all of the errors removed. We accomplish this by defining $\hat{\delta}$ as a projection of α as follows:

$$\hat{\delta} = project(\delta, bit \neq error).$$

Proof of

$$\exists n \left(|X| = n \quad \wedge \quad \alpha = < M_i^+ >_{i=1}^{n-1} < M_n^{\bullet} > \right) \tag{A1}$$

$P1$ is the loop invariant. It is true when the loop is first entered, and if it is true when the loop body is begun, then it is true upon completion of the loop body. In this presentation, we collapse portions of the code that do not affect the invariant into ellipses.

$$< d_i >_{i=1}^{0} = empty\ sequence$$

n is an auxiliary variable

$$P1 \equiv \left(|X| = n \wedge \alpha = < M_i^+ >_{i=1}^{n} \wedge (|X| > 0 \supset data = X_n) \right)$$

$$P2 \equiv \left(|X| = n - 1 \wedge \alpha = < M_i^+ >_{i=1}^{n-1} \right)$$

$$P3 \equiv \left(|X| = n > 0 \wedge \alpha = < M_i^+ >_{i=1}^{n-1} data = X_n \right)$$

$$P1 \vee P2 \vee P3 \quad \supset \quad A1$$

```
WaitingForAck := 1
LastSent := 0    {n := 0}
{P1 ∧ LastSent ≠ WaitingForAck}
loop
       {P1 ∧ (|X| = 0 ⊃ LastSent ≠ WaitingForAck) }
       if LastSent ≠ WaitingForAck then
             {P1}
             LastSent := LastSent ⊕ 1    {n := n + 1}
             {P2}
             data := X̄.read
             {P3}
       fi
       { (P1 ∨ P3) ∧ |X|>0}
       mab.send(LastSent, data)
       {P1 ∧ |X|>0}
       ...
       {P1 ∧ |X|>0}
end loop
```

Figure 6.4-4
Proof of A1

6.4. The Alternating Bit Protocol

A projection of a history on a boolean expression creates a new history that contains only those elements for which the boolean expression is true. The order of the elements of the original sequence is preserved in the projected sequence. The new sequence $\hat{\delta}$ has only the acknowledgments with *bit* equal to 0 or 1. We can define $\#(\hat{\delta}, i)$ in the same way as $\#(\alpha, i)$. Let the projection take δ_i to $\hat{\delta}_{\pi(i)}$. We can extend $\#$ to δ as follows:

$$\#(\delta, i) = \begin{cases} \#(\hat{\delta}, \pi(i)), & \text{if } \sim corrupted(\delta_i) \\ \#(\delta, i) = \#(\delta, i-1), & \text{if } corrupted(\delta_i), \end{cases}$$

where $\#(\delta, 0) = 0$.

We are now ready to relate the parity changes of α to those of δ. The third invariant for process A states that the ith message is not sent until the $(i-1)^{st}$ acknowledgment has been received:

$$\#(\alpha, |\alpha|) \geq i \quad \supset \quad \#(\delta, |\delta|) \geq i - 1. \tag{A3}$$

The fourth invariant compares position i in δ with position $i+1$ in α:

$$\forall i \leq (|\alpha| - 1)\, (\#(\alpha, i+1) = \#(\delta, i) + 1). \tag{A4}$$

Safety: Process B

In process B, γ corresponds to α (of A) in the sense that neither history can contain corrupted messages. We define $\#(\gamma, i)$ in the same way that we defined $\#(\alpha, i)$. The first invariants of the two processes also correspond. Define A_i as the pair $[i \bmod 2, \text{"ack"}]$. Process B's first invariant can be stated as

$$\exists n \left(|Y| = n \wedge \gamma = < A_0^\bullet > < A_i^+ >_{i=1}^{n-1} < A_n^\bullet > \right). \tag{B1}$$

The history β (of B) corresponds to δ (of A) because both can contain corrupted messages. All of the messages in β are in the form $[bit, data]$, where *bit* is an element of $\{0, 1, error\}$. The second invariant relates the length of β to that of γ:

$$|\gamma| \leq |\beta| \leq |\gamma| + 1. \tag{B2}$$

We define $\hat{\beta}$ in a similar way to $\hat{\delta}$, and then define $\#(\beta, i)$ in a similar way to $\#(\delta, i)$. The third invariant states that the ith datum is not output to Y until

6.4. The Alternating Bit Protocol

i sequence changes have been observed in β. More precisely, we write

$$|Y| \geq i \quad \supset \quad \#(\beta, |\beta|) \geq i. \tag{B3}$$

The fourth invariant corresponds to A4:

$$\forall i \leq |\gamma| \left(\#(\gamma, i) = \#(\beta, i)\right). \tag{B4}$$

Our goal is to prove the correct transfer of data from X to Y. We must, therefore, make an assertion for process B that relates the data in β to the contents of Y. Our assertion is the following: every element of Y corresponds to a non-corrupted element of β, such that the data values are the same and the position of the element in Y equals the sequence number of the element of β. The precise definition is

$$\forall i \leq |Y| \left(\exists j \leq |\beta| \left(\sim corrupted(\beta_j) \wedge Y_i = \beta_j.data \wedge i = \#(\beta, j)\right)\right). \tag{B5}$$

An intuitive justification of B5 is based on the observation that process B only adds a new element to Y when it detects a non-corrupted message with a sequence bit different from the last non-corrupted message. If such a new message is found, then the value added to Y is exactly the data contents of the new message.

Safety: System

We now have all the invariants necessary to prove the system invariant:

$$Y \preceq X. \tag{S1}$$

This invariant states that the output values are some initial sequence of the input values. It does not imply that any output values are ever produced; that requirement is given in the liveness specifications to be discussed later.

We proceed by assuming the invariants for the two processes and the communication media, and showing that S1 must follow.

6.4. The Alternating Bit Protocol

▶**Proof of S1** (outline):

We first prove the following system invariant:

$$\forall i \leq |\beta| \left(\sim corrupted(\beta_i) \quad \supset \quad (\alpha_i = \beta_i \quad \wedge \quad \#(\alpha_i) = \#(\beta_i)) \right). \quad (S2)$$

After we have proved the validity of S2, we can combine S2 with B5 to obtain

$$\forall i \leq |Y| \left(\exists j \leq |\alpha| \, (Y_i = \alpha_j.\text{data} \quad \wedge \quad i = \#(\alpha, j)) \right).$$

Using A1 we can re-write this last formula in terms of X_i:

$$\forall i \leq |Y| \, (Y_i = X_i),$$

which implies

$$Y \preceq X. \qquad\qquad\qquad \blacksquare$$

We shall now show that S2 is true; that will imply that S1 is true.

▶**Proof of S2**:

The first half of the conclusion is trivial. Invariant mab2 implies immediately that if an element of β is not corrupted, then its data value must equal that of the corresponding element of α. In other words, the medium guarantees that

$$\forall i \leq |\beta| \, (\sim corrupted(\beta_i) \quad \supset \quad \alpha_i = \beta_i). \qquad (1)$$

We must prove, therefore, that the sequence numbers correspond:

$$\forall i \leq |\beta| \, (\sim corrupted(\beta_i) \quad \supset \quad \#(\alpha, i) = \#(\beta, i)). \qquad (2)$$

The proof involves showing the possible relationships between the two sequence numbers. We compute the relationships in two ways: using assertions about the mab medium and using assertions about the mba medium. The result will be that the only relationship that can exist with both sets of assertions is equality.

Consider a sequence of zeros and ones. We selectively corrupt elements of this sequence. Each time an element is corrupted, the # value of every element of the sequence either remains the same or decreases; Figure 6.4–5 shows all possible configurations of three elements and the resulting parity values when the middle element is corrupted. Note that for all non-corrupted elements of the sequence, the difference in the parity values before and after corrupting any element (except the last) must be even.

There are sixteen possible configurations of three elements where any element can be 0 or 1, the first element can be ⊢ (the beginning of the sequence), and the last element can be ⊣ (the end of the sequence). Corruptions will be represented by changing the middle element of the configuration to E (error). The effect on the sequence numbers (#) is shown below the sequence.

original	⊢ 0 0	⊢ 0 1	⊢ 1 0	⊢ 1 1
#	0 0	0 1	1 2	1 1
corrupted	⊢ E 0	⊢ E 1	⊢ E 0	⊢ E 1
#	0 0	0 1	0 0	0 1

original	0 0 0	0 0 1	0 1 0	0 1 1
#	i i i	i i $i+1$	i $i+1$ $i+2$	i $i+1$ $i+1$
corrupted	0 E 0	0 E 1	0 E 0	0 E 1
#	i i i	i i $i+1$	i i i	i i $i+1$

original	1 0 0	1 0 1	1 1 0	1 1 1
#	i $i+1$ $i+1$	i $i+1$ $i+2$	i i $i+1$	i i i
corrupted	1 E 0	1 E 1	1 E 0	1 E 1
#	i i $i+1$	i i i	i i $i+1$	i i i

original	0 0 ⊣	0 1 ⊣	1 0 ⊣	1 1 ⊣
#	i i	i $i+1$	i $i+1$	i i
corrupted	0 E ⊣	0 E ⊣	1 E ⊣	1 E ⊣
#	i i	i i	i i	i i

Figure 6.4–5
Parity and Corruption

6.4. The Alternating Bit Protocol

We can consider β to be formed from α by this corruption process (the data value are not affected). Because each corruption either decreases the sequence number of an element or leaves the sequence number alone, we can write

$$\forall i \leq |\beta| \, (\#(\beta, i) \leq \#(\alpha, i)). \tag{S3}$$

Similar reasoning with δ and γ yields

$$\forall i \leq |\delta| \, (\#(\delta, i) \leq \#(\gamma, i)). \tag{S4}$$

Invariants S3 and S4 will be used in this proof and in the system liveness proof.

We now relate the parity differences in α to those of β through the invariants of γ and δ. Invariant A4 relates the sequence numbers of α to those of δ:

$$\forall i \leq (|\alpha| - 1) \, (\#(\alpha, i + 1) = \#(\delta, i) + 1). \tag{A4}$$

Formula S4 relates δ to γ. Invariant B4 relates the parity changes of γ to those of β:

$$\forall i \leq |\gamma| \, (\#(\gamma, i) = \#(\beta, i)). \tag{B4}$$

Combining these three invariants, we obtain

$$\forall i \leq (|\alpha| - 1) \, (\#(\alpha, i + 1) \leq 1 + \#(\beta, i)).$$

The value of $\#$ on a history is monitonically non-decreasing, therefore

$$\#(\alpha, i) \leq \#(\alpha, i + 1),$$

which allows us to conclude

$$\forall i \leq (|\alpha| - 1) \, (\#(\alpha, i) \leq 1 + \#(\beta, i)). \tag{3}$$

We combine S3 and (3) to obtain

$$\forall i \leq (|\alpha| - 1) \, (\#(\alpha, i) - 1 \leq \#(\beta, i) \leq \#(\alpha, i)). \tag{4}$$

But, we know that for non-corrupted messages (excluding the last message) in β the difference in the corresponding sequence numbers must be even. Therefore, formula (4) implies

$$\forall i \leq (|\alpha| - 1) \, (\sim corrupted(\beta_i) \supset \#(\beta, i) = \#(\alpha, i)). \tag{5}$$

All that remains is to change (5) to range over the length of β; we would then have proved (2), and hence S2. Invariant mab3 implies that either $|\alpha| = |\beta|$ or $|\alpha| - 1 = |\beta|$. In the second case, (5) is equivalent to (2). In the first case, the definition of $\#$ implies that if $\beta_{|\beta|}$ is not corrupted, then $\#(\beta, |\beta|) = \#(\alpha, |\beta|)$. ∎.

6.4. The Alternating Bit Protocol

A similar proof would show that the parity changes for uncorrupted messages of δ are the same as the corresponding messages of γ:

$$\forall i \leq |\delta|\,(\sim corrupted(\delta_i) \quad \supset \quad \#(\gamma, i) = \#(\delta, i)). \tag{S5}$$

Liveness: Process A

Now let us consider the liveness specifications of process A. They consist of five commitments. First, if conditions are right, the output history α grows without bound:

$$\square\diamond mab.empty \wedge \square\diamond mba.full \quad \supset \quad u(\alpha). \tag{A5}$$

We justify A5 by noting that if there is no blocking, then one message is sent on each cycle of the loop.

The second commitment for process A is a direct result of invariant A2:

$$u(\alpha) \equiv u(\delta). \tag{A6}$$

Because $|\alpha|$ and $|\delta|$ are related by A2, if either one increases without bound, then so must the other.

The third commitment is a promise to start sending the next data item as soon as the current one has been acknowledged:

$$\forall i \left(\#(\delta, |\delta|) \geq i \supset |X| \geq i \right) \wedge u(\alpha) \quad \supset$$
$$\forall j \left(\#(\delta, |\delta|) \geq j \supset \left(uc(\alpha, M_{j+1}) \vee \diamond(\#(\delta, |\delta|) \geq j+1) \right) \right) \tag{A7}$$

The first clause of the hypothesis of A7 is an assertion that the rest of the system must satisfy: an acknowledgment for message i is not received before process A has started to work on message i, and the length of α increases without bound. Under that assumption, if process A receives acknowledgment j, then A starts to send message $j+1$; it will send that message an unbounded number of times unless it eventually receives acknowledgment $j+1$.

The final two commitments relate α to δ in the case of deadlock:

$$\diamond\square(mab.full) \wedge \square\diamond(mba.full) \quad \supset \quad \diamond\square(|\alpha| = |\delta|), \tag{A8}$$
$$\diamond\square(mba.empty) \wedge \square\diamond(mab.empty) \quad \supset \quad \diamond\square(|\alpha| = |\delta| + 1). \tag{A9}$$

An outline of the proof of A8 is shown in Figure 6.4-6. The proof of A9 is similar.

Proof of

$$\Diamond\Box(mab.full) \wedge \Box\Diamond(mba.full) \supset \Diamond\Box(|\alpha| = |\delta|) \qquad (A8)$$

In order to prove A8, we first show that

$$at\ mab.send \supset |\alpha| = |\delta|. \qquad (1)$$

▶**Proof of (1):**

    A: process
        $\{\ |\alpha|=|\delta|=0\ \}$
        loop
            $\{\ |\alpha|=|\delta|\ \}$
            ...
            $\{\ |\alpha|=|\delta|\ \}$
            $mab.send(\ LastSent,\ data)$ $\{\ does\ not\ change\ |\delta|\ \}$
            $\{\ |\alpha|=|\delta|+1\ \}$
            $mba.receive(\ ackno,\ ack)$ $\{\ does\ not\ change\ |\alpha|\ \}$
            $\{\ |\alpha|=|\delta|\ \}$
            ...
            $\{\ |\alpha|=|\delta|\ \}$
        end loop
    end process ■

Invariant mab5 implies

$$A\ at\ mab.send \wedge |\alpha| = |\delta| \wedge \Box(\sim mab.empty) \quad \supset \quad \Box(|\alpha| = |\delta|).$$

Invariant mab1, mab5, and formula (1) together imply

$$A\ at\ mab.send \wedge \Box(mab.full) \supset \Box(|\alpha| = |\delta|). \qquad (2)$$

If (2) is *always* true, then (2) is *eventually* true:

$$\Diamond(A\ at\ mab.send \wedge \Box(mab.full) \supset \Box(|\alpha| = |\delta|)). \qquad (3)$$

Distributing the $\Diamond$ over (3) where legal (see Appendix A), we obtain

$$\Diamond(A\ at\ mab.send) \wedge \Diamond\Box(mab.full) \supset \Diamond\Box(|\alpha| = |\delta|). \qquad (4)$$

If $\Box\Diamond(mba.full)$, then $mba.receive$ cannot block. Therefore, if control is anywhere inside the loop, then it eventually reaches at $mab.send$. That implies, with (4) that

$$\Box\Diamond(mba.full) \wedge \Diamond\Box(mab.full) \supset \Diamond\Box(|\alpha| = |\delta|). \qquad ■$$

Figure 6.4–6
Proof of A8

6.4. The Alternating Bit Protocol

Liveness: Process B

Next consider the liveness specifications of process B. Again we have five commitments, and they are similar to the commitments of process A. First, process B will cause the lengths of β and γ to grow without bound as long as there are no *send* or *receive* operations that fail to terminate:

$$\Box\Diamond mba.empty \wedge \Box\Diamond mab.full \quad \supset \quad u(\beta). \tag{B6}$$

The length of the histories β and δ are related by B2, which implies

$$u(\beta) \equiv u(\gamma). \tag{B7}$$

The third commitment states that B will acknowledge each message it receives:

$$\forall i \left(\#(\beta, |\beta|) \geq i \supset |Y| \geq i-1 \right) \wedge u(\beta) \quad \supset$$
$$\forall j \left(\#(\beta, |\beta|) \geq j \supset \left(\Diamond(|Y| \geq j) \wedge \left(uc(\gamma, A_j) \vee \Diamond(\#(\beta, |\beta|) \geq j+1) \right) \right) \right) \tag{B8}$$

This is analogous to commitment A7; the hypothesis must be satisfied by the rest of the system.

The final two commitments relate β to γ in the case of deadlock:

$$\Diamond\Box(mab.empty) \wedge \Box\Diamond(mba.empty) \quad \supset \quad \Diamond\Box(|\beta| = |\gamma|), \tag{B9}$$

$$\Diamond\Box(mba.full) \wedge \Box\Diamond(mab.full) \quad \supset \quad \Diamond\Box(|\beta| = |\gamma| + 1). \tag{B10}$$

The proofs of B9 and B10 are similar to the proof of A8 in Figure 6.4–6.

Liveness: no starvation

System invariant S1 states that if any output comes out on Y, then it is the same as the input that went in on X. The liveness property that we want to prove is that the length of the output history increases without bound:

$$u(Y). \tag{S6}$$

Our first step in establishing S6 is a proof that all history variables of the media grow without bound:

$$u(\alpha) \wedge u(\beta) \wedge u(\gamma) \wedge u(\delta). \tag{S7}$$

6.4. The Alternating Bit Protocol

▶**Proof of S7:**

We first show that if any of the four history variables grows without bound, then they all do. We then show that one of the histories must grow without bound.

The following four commitments prove that if any of α, β, γ, and δ grow without bound, then they all do:

$$u(\alpha) \equiv u(\delta) \qquad \text{(A6)}$$
$$u(\beta) \equiv u(\gamma) \qquad \text{(B7)}$$
$$|\beta| \le |\alpha| \le |\beta| + 1 \qquad \text{(mab3)}$$
$$|\delta| \le |\gamma| \le |\delta| + 1. \qquad \text{(mba3)}$$

In combination, these assertions imply

$$u(\alpha) \equiv u(\beta) \equiv u(\gamma) \equiv u(\delta). \qquad (1)$$

We prove by contradiction that $u(\alpha)$ grows without bound. Suppose that $\sim u(\alpha)$. Formula (1) then implies that β does not grow without bound, $\sim u(\beta)$. Under what conditions can this happen? The contrapositives of A6 and B6 give us the answer:

$$\sim(\Box\Diamond mab.empty \land \Box\Diamond mba.full) \quad \land \quad \sim(\Box\Diamond mba.empty \land \Box\Diamond mab.full). \quad (2)$$

Rewriting (2) using mab1 and mba1, we obtain

$$(\Diamond\Box mab.full \lor \Diamond\Box mba.empty) \quad \land \quad (\Diamond\Box mba.full \lor \Diamond\Box mab.empty) \qquad (3)$$

as the condition for blocking the increase of α. We can further rearrange formula (3) and eliminate some contradictory clauses:

$$(\Diamond\Box mab.full \land \Diamond\Box mba.full) \quad \lor \quad (\Diamond\Box mab.empty \land \Diamond\Box mba.empty),$$

which is equivalent to

$$\Diamond\Box(mab.full \land mba.full) \quad \lor \quad \Diamond\Box(mab.empty \land mba.empty). \qquad (4)$$

We recast (4) in terms of the lengths of the media histories by using mab3, mba3, A8, A9, B9, and B10. The resulting condition for blocking α is

$$\Diamond\Box(|\alpha| = |\beta| + 1 \land |\gamma| = |\delta| + 1 \land |\alpha| = |\delta| \land |\beta| = |\gamma| + 1) \quad \lor$$
$$\Diamond\Box(|\alpha| = |\beta| \land |\gamma| = |\delta| \land |\alpha| = |\delta| + 1 \land |\beta| = |\gamma|).$$

The first clause implies

$$|\alpha| = |\beta| + 1 = |\gamma| + 2 = |\delta| + 3 = |\alpha| + 3.$$

The second clause implies

$$|\alpha| = |\delta| + 1 = |\gamma| + 1 = |\beta| + 1 = |\alpha| + 1.$$

Both clauses imply contradictions; therefore $u(\alpha)$ is true. Formula (1) and $u(\alpha)$ imply S7. ∎

6.4. The Alternating Bit Protocol

Liveness: System

The system liveness property we want to prove is that each message is eventually output. Because S1 tells us that any output produced is an initial segment of the input sequence, all we need to establish is that the length of the output history grows without bound:

$$u(Y). \qquad (S6)$$

We prove S6 by induction on the length of Y. The base step is to show $\diamond(|Y| \geq 0)$, which is true initially. The induction step involves showing that if Y contains k messages at some point, then it will eventually contain $k+1$ messages:

$$\square(|Y| = k \supset \diamond|Y| > k).$$

▶**Proof of** S6:

The first step in the proof is to establish the hypotheses of assertions A7 and B8, which state that messages and acknowledgments do not arrive before the recipient is ready to handle them. This is actually a safety property of the system; it often turns out that liveness proofs require additional safety properties. It can be proved easily from the safety specifications of the modules.

$$
\begin{array}{lll}
\#(\delta, |\delta|) \geq i & \supset \quad \#(\gamma, |\gamma|) \geq i & (S4) \\
& \supset \quad |Y| \geq i & (B1) \\
& \supset \quad \#(\beta, |\beta|) \geq i & (B3) \\
& \supset \quad \#(\alpha, |\alpha|) \geq i & (S3) \\
& \supset \quad |X| \geq i & (A1) \\
& \supset \quad \#(\delta, |\delta|) \geq i-1 & (A3) \\
& \supset \quad \#(\gamma, |\gamma|) \geq i-1 & (S4) \\
& \supset \quad |Y| \geq i-1 & (B1)
\end{array}
$$

This implies both hypotheses:

$$\#(\delta, |\delta|) \geq i \quad \supset \quad |X| \geq i$$

and

$$\#(\beta, |\beta|) \geq i \quad \supset \quad |Y| \geq i-1.$$

We now know that the conclusions of A7 and B8 hold, so we can reason with the simpler forms:

$$\forall j \left(\#(\delta, |\delta|) \geq j \supset \left(uc(\alpha, M_{j+1}) \vee \diamond(\#(\delta, |\delta|) \geq j+1) \right) \right) \qquad (A7')$$

6.4. The Alternating Bit Protocol

$$\forall j\left(\#(\beta, |\beta|) \geq j \supset \left(\diamond(|Y| \geq j) \wedge \left(uc(\gamma, A_j) \vee \diamond\left(\#(\beta, |\beta|) \geq j+1\right)\right)\right)\right) \quad (B8')$$

To prove the induction step, suppose that at some point $|Y| = k$. Then, applying $B8'$, either

$$uc(\gamma, A_k), \text{ or} \tag{1}$$

$$\diamond\left(\#(\beta, |\beta|) \geq k+1\right) \tag{2}$$

is true.

We can show with mab4, mba4, and our system safety properties that the following two system commitments are true:

$$\#(\alpha, |\alpha|) \geq i \wedge uc(\alpha, M_i) \supset \diamond\left(\#(\beta, |\beta|) \geq i\right)$$

and

$$\#(\gamma, |\gamma|) \geq i \wedge uc(\gamma, A_i) \supset \diamond\left(\#(\delta, |\delta|) \geq i\right).$$

Case (1) implies

$$\diamond(\#(\delta, |\delta|) \geq k).$$

Using $A7'$ this formula in turn implies

$$uc(\alpha, M_{k+1}), \text{ or} \tag{1a}$$

$$\diamond\left(\#(\delta, |\delta|) \geq k+1\right). \tag{1b}$$

Now case (1a) implies

$$\diamond\left(\#(\beta, |\beta|) \geq k+1\right).$$

Therefore case (1a) reduces to case (2). But case 2 implies $\diamond|Y| \geq k+1$ (using $B8'$). Finally, the system safety relations proved above show that case (1b) implies $\diamond|Y| \geq k+1$. This completes the induction step and the proof of S6.

∎

6.5.   Stenning's Data Transfer Protocol (Simplified Version)

Much of the detail in the proof of the alternating bit protocol is a result of having only a single bit per message for sequencing. Relaxing the constraint to permit integers for sequence numbers allows for a protocol that is similar in complexity to the alternating bit protocol, but is able to cope with a much less reliable medium. The resulting correctness proof is also simpler. In this section, we discuss a simplified version of a data transfer protocol presented by Stenning [43, 44]. Stenning verified the safety properties of his algorithm, using a non-modular proof technique. He did not consider liveness, and it is possible for his algorithm to enter an infinite loop and fail to deliver messages. In the version presented here, that fault has been repaired, and we give a proof of the algorithm's liveness.

Figure 6.5–1 illustrates the network structure. The code for the simplified Stenning protocol is given in Figures 6.5–2 and 6.5–3. The full protocol is discussed and proved in Section 6.6. The code consists of two processes: a transmitter and a receiver. The transmitter takes as input an unbounded sequence of messages from source $\overline{X}$. The associated history is X. The transmitter sends the data to the receiver via communication medium mtr. The receiver outputs messages to sink $\overline{Y}$, with associated output sequence Y, and acknowledges receipt via communication medium mrt. Complications arise because the communication media are unreliable. Messages can be lost, duplicated, or reordered. (We assume that message corruption, if it can occur, is detected by a lower level checksum mechanism and that corrupted messages are discarded.)

The protocol must ensure that the messages are ultimately delivered correctly in spite of this unreliability. This is accomplished by attaching a sequence number to each message sent by the transmitter and to each acknowledgment sent by the receiver. The transmitter sends each message repeatedly until it receives an acknowledgment of that message, using a timeout mechanism to trigger the retransmission. The first time the receiver gets a message with a given sequence number, it records the message in the output stream. It also sends an acknowledgment to the transmitter for every message it receives.

Communication Medium

Section 6.3 discussed the communications medium used by this protocol. The assertions, as applied to this protocol, are listed below.

The medium's first invariant states that nothing comes out that was not put in:

$$m \in \beta \quad \supset \quad m \in \alpha \qquad\qquad\qquad (mtr1)$$

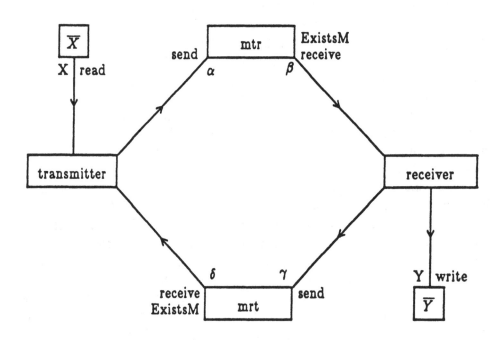

Figure 6.5-1
Stenning's Data Transfer Protocol

```
Transmitter: process
var
        WaitingForAck, HighestSent: integer
        data, ack: item
        ackno: integer
        α, δ, X: private history
begin
        { initialize }
        WaitingForAck := 1
        HighestSent := 0

        loop
                { send message }
                if HighestSent < WaitingForAck then
                        HighestSent := HighestSent + 1
                        data := X̄.read
                        mtr.send( [ HighestSent, data] )
                        timer.start
                fi

                { service acknowledgments }
                if mrt.ExistsM then
                        mrt.receive( [ ackno,ack] )
                        if ackno = WaitingForAck then
                                timer.cancel
                                WaitingForAck := ackno + 1
                        fi
                fi

                { service time-outs }
                if timer.timedout then
                        timer.cancel
                        mtr.send( [ HighestSent, data] )
                        timer.start
                fi
        end loop
end process
```

Figure 6.5-2

Stenning's Data Transfer Protocol: Transmitter

```
Receiver: process
var
        NextRequired: integer
        messno: integer
        info: item
        β, γ, Y: private history
begin

        { initialize }
        NextRequired := 1

        loop

                { get message }
                mtr.receive( [ messno, info] )

                if messno = NextRequired then
                        { service new message }
                        Y̅.write( info )
                        NextRequired := NextRequired + 1
                fi

                { send acknowledgment }
                mrt.send( [ NextRequired - 1, "ack"] )

        end loop

end process
```

Figure 6.5–3
Stenning's Data Transfer Protocol: Receiver

6.5. Stenning's Data Transfer Protocol (Simplified Version)

$$m \in \delta \quad \supset \quad m \in \gamma, \qquad\qquad (mrt1)$$

where m is any message. The medium can lose, duplicate, and re-order messages, but it does not create spurious messages. These invariants are weaker than assertions mab2 and mba2 in the alternating bit protocol: mtr1 and mrt1 only specify the existence of a source message, not its exact position in the source history. This weakening is allowable because the identifying sequence numbers come from the sequence information of the message, rather than from the position of the message in the history.

The first commitment is as follows. If an unbounded number of messages are sent, then messages are infinitely often available to be received:

$$u(\alpha) \quad \supset \quad \Box\Diamond(mtr.ExistsM) \qquad\qquad (mtr2)$$

$$u(\gamma) \quad \supset \quad \Box\Diamond(mrt.ExistsM). \qquad\qquad (mrt2)$$

The second commitment asserts that if the same message is sent over and over again, it will eventually be delivered (provided that the receiving process repeatedly accepts messages):

$$(uc(\alpha, m) \wedge u(\beta)) \quad \supset \quad \Diamond m \in \beta \qquad\qquad (mtr3)$$

$$(uc(\gamma, m) \wedge u(\delta)) \quad \supset \quad \Diamond m \in \delta. \qquad\qquad (mrt3)$$

These assertions are similar to mab4 and mba4 in the alternating bit protocol. The assertions above, however, would not be strong enough for that protocol; two different messages can have the same parity and the same data component.

The medium provides three services: send a message, receive a message, and check to see whether any messages are waiting to be received. The specifications of these services are given below for the medium mtr; the services for mrt are essentially the same.

send(m)

    pre: $\alpha = A$
    post: $\alpha = A < m >$
    live: $\Diamond(after\ mtr.send)$

receive(var m)

    pre: $\beta = B$
    post: $\beta = B < m >$
    live: $\Diamond(mtr.ExistsM) \quad \supset \quad \Diamond(after\ mtr.receive)$

6.5. Stenning's Data Transfer Protocol (Simplified Version)

ExistsM

  pre: *true*
  post: *true*
  live: $\diamond$(after mtr.ExistsM)

Note that a *send* operation always terminates, and *receive* terminates if a message is available. The pre- and post-conditions of *ExistsM* are both true, which gives no safety information about the operation. The *ExistsM* function is not involved in the safe operation of the protocol. It is used only to guarantee that the *receive* operation will terminate (a liveness property).

The live-assertion for *receive* contains a hidden assumption about the operation of *ExistsM*. Our intuitive definition of *ExistsM* said that the function is true if there is a message to be received. Because there is only one receiver, if *ExistsM* becomes true, then it will not become false before a *receive* operation takes place. The additional invariant that describes this property is

$$mtr.ExistsM \wedge \Box(\sim receiver\ after\ mtr.receive) \quad \supset \quad \Box(mtr.ExistsM).$$

The Timer

The timer is another black box, and we define its properties in a similar way. The timer has three mutually exclusive states that are visible to the calling process: *running*, *stopped*, and *timedout*. The most important statement about the timer is its commitment: if the timer is set and never cancelled, then eventually there will be a timeout notification.

The timer provides two auxiliary functions that correspond to the states *running* and *stopped*. The state *timedout* is exported through a visible function. Initially the timer is in the *stopped* state. We specify the states as follows:

$$
\begin{aligned}
stopped &\quad \supset \quad \sim running \wedge \sim timedout \\
running &\quad \supset \quad \sim stopped \wedge \sim timedout \\
timedout &\quad \supset \quad \sim stopped \wedge \sim running.
\end{aligned}
$$

The liveness commitment is the vital assertion mentioned above:

$$running \wedge \Box(\sim stopped) \quad \supset \quad \diamond(timedout).$$

There are three services that the timer provides: start the timer, cancel the timer, and determine if the timer has timedout. The pre- and post-assertions of all three services are true; all three services are used only to guarantee that the caller is live.

6.5. Stenning's Data Transfer Protocol (Simplified Version)

start

   live: *stopped* ⊃   ◇(*after timer.start*) ∧ ◇(*running*)

cancel

   live: ◇(*after timer.cancel* ∧ *stopped*)

timedout

   live: ◇(*after timer.timedout*)

As with the medium services, these timer services conceal some hidden assumptions. We assume that only one process has access to the timer; it is not shared. We also constrain the *stopped* state not to change unless *start* is called, and *timedout* will not change unless *cancel* is called:

$$stopped \wedge \Box(\sim after\ start) \supset \Box(stopped)$$

$$timedout \wedge \Box(\sim after\ cancel) \supset \Box(timedout).$$

Safety: Transmitter and Receiver

A message consists of the pair i and X_i; we abbreviate $[i, X_i]$ by M_i. This is the form of messages in α and β. An acknowledgment for message i, the pair $[i, \text{"ack"}]$, is denoted by A_i; messages in γ and δ have this form.

The safety specification of the transmitter consists of two invariants.

$$\exists n \left(|X| = n \quad \wedge \quad \alpha = < M_i^{+} >_{i=1}^{n-1} < M_n^{*} > \right) \tag{T1}$$

$$|X| \geq k \quad \supset \quad A_{k-1} \in \delta \tag{T2}$$

The first invariant states that when n items have been input to the transmitter, the output to the *mtr* medium is a sequence of repeated messages. The last term is M_n^{*}, rather than M_n^{+}, because just after the operation $\overline{X}.read$ in the transmitter, the nth piece of data has been read in, but message M_n has not yet been sent.

The invariant T2 states that the kth input item is not read until after the acknowledgment for the $(k-1)^{st}$ message has been received.

6.5. Stenning's Data Transfer Protocol (Simplified Version)

The receiver has two invariants that are similar to those of the transmitter

$$m \in \beta \supset \exists j \, (m = M_j) \quad \supset$$
$$\exists n \, (Y \preceq < X_i >_{i=1}^{n}) \quad \wedge \quad |Y| \geq k \supset M_k \in \beta, \tag{R1}$$

$$A_i \in \gamma \quad \supset \quad (M_i \in \beta \wedge |Y| \geq i) \tag{R2}$$

Invariant R1 states that the receiver output Y will be legitimate if its input β is legitimate. More precisely, if β contains only messages of the form $[i, X_i]$, then Y will be a sequence of data items $< X_i >_{i=1}^{n}$; each datum in Y must correspond to a message that appears in β. To verify that the receiver satisfies this invariant, observe that the receiver will add the ith element to Y only after it receives a message with sequence number i, and the value that is appended to Y is the one contained in the message. Because each message in β has the form $[i, X_i]$, the ith element of Y must be X_i.

The second invariant states that if acknowledgment i is in the output history γ, then message i is in the input history β, and the associated datum X_i is in Y. This is obvious from the flow of control in the receiver. An acknowledgment is only sent after the corresponding message has been received and its datum appended to Y.

Safety: System

The system safety specification is the same as invariant S1 of the alternating bit protocol:

$$Y \preceq X. \tag{S1}$$

▶**Proof of S1:**

As a first step in proving S1, we note that the hypothesis of the receiver assertion R1,

$$m \in \beta \quad \supset \quad \exists j (m = M_j),$$

follows immediately from the safety properties of the transmitter and the medium *mtr*. Because the transmitter only puts legitimate messages into the medium (T1), and any message that comes out of the medium must have been put in by the transmitter (mtr1), the receiver can only obtain legitimate messages.

Now let

$$n = \max\{i : M_i \in \beta\}.$$

6.5.   Stenning's Data Transfer Protocol (Simplified Version)

Because the hypothesis of R1 is satisfied, we know that the conclusion of R1 holds, namely

$$Y \preceq < X_i >_{i=1}^n .$$

By R1, each X_i in Y comes from a message m in β. Invariant mtr1 implies that the messages in β correspond to messages in α:

$$M_n \in \beta \quad \supset \quad M_n \in \alpha.$$

Invariant T1 relates the messages in α to the data in X:

$$M_n \in \alpha \quad \supset \quad < X_i >_{i=1}^n \preceq X.$$

Thus we can conclude

$$Y \preceq < X_i >_{i=1}^n \preceq X,$$

which implies invariant S1. ∎

Liveness: Transmitter and Receiver

The transmitter has three liveness commitments. First, the transmitter output history α grows without bound:

$$u(\alpha). \tag{T3}$$

This commitment is independent of any assumptions about the environment. To see that it is valid, we note that the transmitter code is a repeating loop that can never be blocked: the only operation that can cause blocking is *receive*, and *receive* is performed only when an acknowledgment is known to be available. If there were no timeout mechanism, then the loop could cycle forever with no messages being sent. The timer assertions, however, allow us to conclude that if the timer is not cancelled, then eventually *timedout* will be true. Therefore, even if the first two if statements of the loop are never executed, the third if statement will be executed infinitely often—and a message will be sent.

The second transmitter commitment is

$$\Box\Diamond(mrt.ExistsM) \quad \supset \quad u(\delta) \tag{T4}$$

This commitment states that the transmitter will increase the size of δ provided that the environment keeps making acknowledgments available in *mrt*. This

6.5. Stenning's Data Transfer Protocol (Simplified Version)

follows from the absence of blocking, and the fact that the transmitter will accept an acknowledgment each time around its loop, if one is available.

The third commitment is a promise to start sending the next data item as soon as the current one has been acknowledged.

$$\forall i \, (A_i \in \delta \supset |X| \geq i) \supset$$
$$\forall j \, (A_j \in \delta \supset (uc(\alpha, M_{j+1}) \lor \Diamond(A_{j+1} \in \delta))) \tag{T5}$$

The hypothesis of this commitment is an assertion that the rest of the system must satisfy: an acknowledgment for message i is not received before the transmitter has started to work on message i. Under that assumption, once the transmitter receives acknowledgment j, it starts to send message $j + 1$. It will send that message an unbounded number of times unless it eventually receives acknowledgment $j + 1$.

Next we consider the liveness specifications of the receiver. Again we have three commitments, and they are similar to the commitments of the transmitter. First, the receiver will cause the lengths of β and γ to grow without bound as long as it is able to receive messages from mtr:

$$\Box\Diamond(mtr.ExistsM) \supset u(\gamma) \tag{R3}$$

$$\Box\Diamond(mtr.ExistsM) \supset u(\beta). \tag{R4}$$

The receiver code satisfies these assertions because the repeated availability of messages implies that the receiver cannot be blocked at its *receive* operation. Therefore, it repeatedly executes its loop body, and each time it increases the length of β and γ. Note that the transmitter commitment T3, which corresponds to R3, does not require an assumption about the rest of the system in order to guarantee that the size of α keeps growing. This difference between T3 and R3 comes from the transmitter's use of a timeout mechanism. The receiver's third commitment is to acknowledge each message it receives:

$$\forall i \, (M_i \in \beta \supset |Y| \geq i - 1) \land u(\beta) \supset$$
$$\forall j \left(M_j \in \beta \supset (\Diamond(|Y| \geq j) \land (uc(\gamma, A_j) \lor \Diamond(M_{j+1} \in \beta))) \right). \tag{R5}$$

This commitment is analogous to T5. Assuming that message i does not arrive until the receiver has processed $i - 1$ and that β grows without bound, then the receiver will acknowledge each message it receives until the next one arrives and will add X_k to the output sequence Y. (It is necessary to assume $u(\beta)$ because the receiver can block if messages do not arrive; such an assumption is unnecessary for the transmitter because it can never block.)

Liveness: No Starvation

Our first step in establishing system liveness is a proof that all of the medium history variables grow without bound.

$$
\begin{array}{ll}
u(\alpha) & \text{(T3)} \\
u(\alpha) \supset \Box\Diamond(mtr.ExistsM) & \text{(mtr2)} \\
\Box\Diamond(mtr.ExistsM) \supset u(\gamma) & \text{(R3)} \\
\Box\Diamond(mtr.ExistsM) \supset u(\beta) & \text{(R4)} \\
u(\gamma) \supset \Box\Diamond(mrt.ExistsM) & \text{(mrt2)} \\
\Box\Diamond(mrt.ExistsM) \supset u(\delta) & \text{(R3)}
\end{array}
$$

In combination, these assertions imply that all of the history sequences grow without bound:

$$u(\alpha) \wedge u(\beta) \wedge u(\gamma) \wedge u(\delta).$$

They also imply that input is infinitely often available for *mrt.receive* and *mtr.receive*.

This section of the proof is much simpler than the corresponding part of the alternating bit protocol because the *send* operation cannot be blocked in this model.

Liveness: System

As in the alternating bit protocol, the system liveness property we want to prove is that each message is eventually output:

$$u(Y). \qquad (S2)$$

The proof is similar to the liveness proof of the alternating bit protocol. The proof proceeds by induction on the length of Y. The base step, $\Diamond(|Y| = 0)$, is true initially. The induction step is to show that if Y contains k messages at some point, then it will eventually contain $k+1$ messages:

$$\Box(|Y| = k \supset \Diamond|Y| > k).$$

6.5. Stenning's Data Transfer Protocol (Simplified Version)

▶**Proof of S2:**

First we establish the hypotheses of assertions T5 and R5, which state that messages and acknowledgments do not arrive before the recipient is ready to handle them; this is a safety property of the system.

$$
\begin{aligned}
A_j \in \delta \quad &\supset \quad A_j \in \gamma && \text{(mrt1)}\\
&\supset \quad |Y| \geq j && \text{(R2)}\\
&\supset \quad M_j \in \beta && \text{(R1)}\\
&\supset \quad M_j \in \alpha && \text{(mtr1)}\\
&\supset \quad |X| \geq j && \text{(T1)}\\
&\supset \quad A_{j-1} \in \delta && \text{(T2)}\\
&\supset \quad A_{j-1} \in \gamma && \text{(mrt1)}\\
&\supset \quad |Y| \geq j-1 && \text{(R2)}
\end{aligned}
$$

This implies both hypotheses:

$$A_j \in \delta \quad \supset \quad |X| \geq j$$

and

$$M_j \in \beta \quad \supset \quad |Y| \geq j-1.$$

We now know that the conclusions of T5 and R5 hold, so we can reason with the simpler forms

$$\forall j \left(A_j \in \delta \supset \left(uc(\alpha, M_{j+1}) \vee \Diamond(A_{j+1} \in \delta) \right) \right) \tag{T5'}$$

$$\forall j \left(M_j \in \beta \supset \left(\Diamond(|Y| \geq j) \wedge \left(uc(\gamma, A_j) \vee \Diamond(M_{j+1} \in \beta) \right) \right) \right) \tag{R5'}$$

To prove the induction step, suppose that at some point $|Y| = k$. R5 then implies

$$uc(\gamma, A_k), \text{ or} \tag{1}$$

$$\Diamond M_{k+1} \in \beta. \tag{2}$$

Case (1) implies $\Diamond A_k \in \delta$ (from mrt3), and using $T5'$ this in turn implies

$$uc(\alpha, M_{k+1}), \text{ or} \tag{1a}$$

$$\Diamond A_{k+1} \in \delta. \tag{1b}$$

Case (1a) implies $\Diamond M_{k+1} \in \beta$ (using mtr3), so case (1a) reduces to case (2). But case (2) implies $\Diamond|Y| \geq k+1$ (using $R5'$). Finally, the system safety relations proved above show that case (1b) implies $\Diamond|Y| \geq k+1$. This completes the induction step and the proof of commitment S2. ∎

6.6. Stenning's Data Transfer Protocol (Full Version)

The simplified version of Stenning's data transfer protocol presented in the last section is inefficient. If the medium is reasonably reliable, most messages will get through the first time they are sent. While the transmitter is waiting for an acknowledgment for message k, it could send message $k+1$. If k gets through the medium, $k+1$ would already be on its way. If a message is lost, messages later in the sequence could be discarded by the receiver, or they could be held by the receiver until the lost message is replaced. The full Stenning protocol [43] follows the second approach. The transmitter sends messages with a range of sequence numbers. The receiver can accept messages within a range of sequence numbers (not necessarily the same range as the transmitter's). If an intermediate message is lost, the receiver holds later messages in temporary storage (called a window) until the lost message is retransmitted and received. The transmitter also maintains a window of messages that have been sent but not acknowledged. Relaxing the system in this way improves network efficiency and has little impact on the correctness proof.

Stenning extended this full version of his protocol by using a bounded set of sequence numbers. That extension is not verified in this thesis, but its correctness can be proved using techniques similar to those used for the alternating bit protocol. (See the discussion at the end of this section.)

The code for the full Stenning protocol is given in Figures 6.6–1 and 6.6–2. The timer functions in the code are described below. The network structure is the same as in Figure 6.5–1. The network consists of two processes: a transmitter and a receiver. The transmitter takes as input an unbounded sequence of messages from source $\overline{X}$; with associated history X. The transmitter sends the data to the receiver via communication medium mtr. The receiver outputs messages to sink $\overline{Y}$, with associated output sequence Y, and acknowledges receipt via communication medium mrt. The media are unreliable; messages can be lost, duplicated, or reordered. (We assume that message corruption, if it can occur, is detected by a lower-level checksum mechanism, and that corrupted messages are treated as lost.)

Sequence numbers are attached to the messages and acknowledgments, as in the simplified protocol. We extend the definition of acknowledgment: A_i still represents the pair $[i, \text{"ack"}]$, but we consider any A_j with $j \geq i$ to be an acknowledgment for message i:

$$Ack(i, \gamma) \quad \equiv \quad \exists j \geq i \, (A_j \in \gamma).$$

The definition of $Ack(i, \delta)$ is similar.

6.6. Stenning's Data Transfer Protocol (Full Version)

As mentioned above, windows are maintained in both processes for temporary storage. To describe these windows, we introduce a new data type: *shifting array*. A shifting array has a maximum size and a base value. Any value of the array between *base* and *base + size − 1* can be accessed. A new base is set with a *shift* command. A *shift* can never decrease the base value. After a *shift*, all new entries of the array have value *empty*. This data type implements an unbounded array with a fixed-size access window. We also need one timer for each slot in the transmitter window. The timers are indexed in the same way as the shifting array in order to represent a finite subset of an infinite set of timers.

Communication Medium

The communication medium is the same as the medium in Sections 6.3 and 6.5. The assertions are listed below.

$$m \in \beta \quad \supset \quad m \in \alpha \qquad\qquad (mtr1)$$

$$m \in \delta \quad \supset \quad m \in \gamma \qquad\qquad (mrt1)$$

$$u(\alpha) \quad \supset \quad \square\lozenge(mtr.ExistsM) \qquad\qquad (mtr2)$$

$$u(\gamma) \quad \supset \quad \square\lozenge(mrt.ExistsM) \qquad\qquad (mrt2)$$

$$(uc(\alpha, m) \wedge u(\beta)) \quad \supset \quad \lozenge m \in \beta \qquad\qquad (mtr3)$$

$$(uc(\gamma, m) \wedge u(\delta)) \quad \supset \quad \lozenge m \in \delta \qquad\qquad (mrt3)$$

send(m)

    pre: $\alpha = A$
    post: $\alpha = A < m >$
    live: $\lozenge(after\ mtr.send)$

receive(var m)

    pre: $\beta = B$
    post: $\beta = B < m >$
    live: $\lozenge(mtr.ExistsM) \quad \supset \quad \lozenge(after\ mtr.receive)$

```
Transmitter: process
constant
      tws = { transmit window size ≥ 1 }
var
      LowestUnackd, HighestSent, ackno, timeno: integer
      ack: item
      TWindow: shifting array [ tws] of item
      α, δ, X: private history
begin
      { initialize }
      LowestUnackd := 1
      HighestSent := 0
      TWindow.shift( 1 )
      loop
            { send any permitted messages }
            while HighestSent-LowestUnackd < ( tws-1) do
                  HighestSent := HighestSent + 1
                  TWindow [ HighestSent] := X.read
                  mtr.send( HighestSent, TWindow [ HighestSent] )
                  timer.start( HighestSent)
            od
            { service acknowledgments }
            if mrt.ExistsM then
                  mrt.receive( ackno,ack )
                  if ackno ≥ LowestUnackd then
                        timer.cancel( LowestUnackd,ackno )
                        LowestUnackd := ackno + 1
                        TWindow.shift( LowestUnackd )
                  fi
            fi
            { service time-outs }
            if timer.TimeoutsExist then
                  timer.which( timeno )
                  timer.cancel( timeno, HighestSent )
                  for i ∈ timeno .. HighestSent do
                        mtr.send( i, TWindow [ i] )
                        timer.start( i )
                  od
            fi
      end loop
end process
```

Figure 6.6-1

Stenning's Data Transfer Protocol: Transmitter

```
Receiver: process
constant
      rws = { receive window sise ≥ 1 }
var
      NextRequired, messno: integer
      info: item
      β, γ, Y: private history
      RWindow: shifting array [ rws ] of item
begin
      { initialise }
      NextRequired := 1
      RWindow.shift ( 1 )
      loop
            { get message }
            mtr.receive ( messno, info )

            if NextRequired ≤ messno < NextRequired + rws then
                  if Rwindow [ messno ] = empty then
                        { service new message }
                        RWindow [ messno ] := info

                        { output any permitted messages }
                        while RWindow [ NextRequired ] ≠ empty do
                              Y̅.write ( info )
                              NextRequired := NextRequired + 1
                              RWindow.shift [ NextRequired ]
                        od
                  fi
            fi
            { send acknowledgment }
            mrt.send ( NextRequired - 1, "ack" )
      end loop
end process
```

Figure 6.6-2
Stenning's Data Transfer Protocol: Receiver

6.6.   Stenning's Data Transfer Protocol (Full Version)

ExistsM

    pre: *true*
    post: *true*
    live: $\Diamond(after\ mtr.ExistsM)$

  As in the simplified version, we also assert

  $(mtr.ExistsM) \wedge \Box(\sim receiver\ after\ mtr.receive) \quad \supset \quad \Box(mtr.ExistsM).$

The Timer

   The timer in this version of the protocol is made up of a number of the timers used in the simplified version; *tws* subtimers are used, one for each transmitter window slot. The subtimers have floating indices, similar to the indices of the shifting arrays. Rather than give the details, we shall say that *stopped* subtimers have no index, and the maximum difference between any two indices must be less than *tws* $-$ 1. The timer offers four services: set a subtimer, cancel a range of subtimers, determine if any subtimers are timedout, and return the index of the subtimer that timedout longest ago.

   The safety invariant specifies three mutually exclusive states for each subtimer: *running, stopped,* and *timedout.* Initially, all of the subtimers are *stopped.* The liveness commitment is, for all subtimers i,

  $$running(i) \wedge \Box(\sim stopped(i)) \quad \supset \quad \Diamond(timedout(i)).$$

Each of three states is exported to the proof of the caller by an auxiliary function. Each function name will be the same as the state it represents. We define the visible function *TimeoutsExist* as follows:

  $$TimeoutsExist \quad \equiv \quad \exists i\,(timedout(i)).$$

The timer services are as follows. All pre- and post-assertions not stated are *true.*

start(i)

    pre: $stopped(i)$
    live: $\Diamond(after\ timer.start) \wedge \Diamond(running(i))$

6.6. Stenning's Data Transfer Protocol (Full Version)

cancel(i,j)

   live: $\Diamond\left(\text{after } timer.cancel \wedge \forall k \left(i \leq k \leq j \supset stopped(k)\right)\right)$

TimeoutsExist

   live: $\Diamond(\text{after } timer.TimeoutsExist)$

which(var i)

   live: $TimeoutsExist \supset \Diamond(\text{after } timer.which \wedge timedout(i))$

As with the timer services in the last section, these timer services are based on some assumptions, which must be made explicit. We assume that only one process has access to the timer; it is not shared. We also constrain the *stopped* state not to change unless *start* is called, and *timedout* will not change unless *cancel* is called:

$$stopped(i) \wedge \Box(\sim \text{after } start(i)) \supset \Box(stopped(i))$$

$$timedout(i) \wedge \Box(\sim \text{after } cancel(j, k)) \supset \Box(timedout(i)),$$

where $j \leq i \leq k$.

Safety: Transmitter and Receiver

The correct operation of the shifting array and the timer requires an safety proof that *HighestSent* and *LowestUnackd* are always within the proper range and that no timer operation or array access is called out of range. These invariants and their proofs are obvious.

A message consisting of the pair $[i, X_i]$ will be abbreviated M_i. This is the form of messages in α and β. An acknowledgment for message i, the pair $[i, \text{"ack"}]$, is denoted by A_i; messages in γ and δ have this form.

For convenience, the first invariant of the simple protocol is replaced by two invariants in the full version. The first new invariant states that all messages get their data from X and their sequence numbers from the positions of the data in X. The second new invariant says that no message is sent before all previous messages have been sent:

$$\exists n \left(|X| = n \quad \wedge \quad \forall m \in \alpha \left(\exists j \leq n (m = M_j)\right)\right) \tag{T1}$$

$$M_i \in \alpha \quad \supset \quad \forall j < i (M_j \in \alpha). \tag{T2}$$

6.6. Stenning's Data Transfer Protocol (Full Version)

The second invariant of the simple protocol is no longer needed because the receiver is now able to handle messages out of order.

The receiver has two invariants that are similar to those in the simple protocol:

$$m \in \beta \supset \exists j \, (m = M_j) \quad \supset$$
$$\exists n \, (Y \preceq < X_i >_{i=1}^n) \quad \wedge \quad |Y| \geq k \supset M_k \in \beta) \tag{R1}$$

$$Ack(i, \gamma) \quad \supset \quad (M_i \in \beta \wedge |Y| \geq i). \tag{R2}$$

Safety: System

The system safety specification is the same as in the simple protocol:

$$Y \preceq X. \tag{S1}$$

The system safety proof is the same as for the simple protocol with only one exception. The formula

$$n = \max\{i : M_i \in \beta\}$$

is replaced by

$$n = |Y|.$$

The substitution is necessary because in the simple version of the protocol any received message can appear in Y. In this version, only those messages received while their sequence numbers were within the receive window can appear in Y.

Liveness: Transmitter and Receiver

The liveness commitments are similar to those in the simple protocol, with the exception of R5. The transmitter commitments are as follows:

$$u(\alpha), \tag{T3}$$

$$\Box \Diamond (mrt.ExistsM) \quad \supset \quad u(\delta), \tag{T4}$$

and

$$\forall i \, (Ack(i, \delta) \supset |X| \geq i) \quad \supset$$
$$\forall j \left(Ack(j, \delta) \supset \left(uc(\alpha, M_{j+1}) \vee \Diamond \big(Ack(j+1, \delta) \big) \right) \right). \tag{T5}$$

6.6. Stenning's Data Transfer Protocol (Full Version)

The first two commitments of the receiver are

$$\Box\Diamond(mtr.ExistsM \;\supset\; u(\gamma)) \tag{R3}$$

and

$$\Box\Diamond(mtr.ExistsM \;\supset\; u(\beta)). \tag{R4}$$

We split the receiver's third commitment into two parts:

$$(u(\beta) \wedge |Y| = j \wedge |\beta| = k) \;\supset\; (uc(\gamma, A_j) \vee \Diamond(\exists i \geq k\,(\beta_i = M_{j+1}))) \tag{R5}$$

$$|Y| = j \wedge |\beta| = k \wedge \Diamond(\exists i \geq k\,(\beta_i = M_{j+1})) \;\supset\; \Diamond(|Y| \geq j+1). \tag{R6}$$

Commitment R5 states that if all of the messages up to and including j have been output, then either acknowledgment j will be sent an unbounded number of times, or message $j + 1$ will be received. R6 describes the effect of message $j + 1$ becoming available: eventually the length of the output grows to $j + 1$. R5 is contingent on the receiver not blocking.

Liveness: No Starvation

The proof that the four histories grow without bound,

$$u(\alpha) \wedge u(\beta) \wedge u(\gamma) \wedge u(\delta),$$

is the same as in the simple protocol.

Liveness: System

The system liveness property we want to prove is that each message is eventually output:

$$u(Y) \tag{S2}.$$

The proof follows the same lines as the proof of the simple protocol. We prove S2 by induction on the length of Y. The induction step is to show that if Y contains k messages at some point, then it will eventually contain $k + 1$ messages.

6.6. Stenning's Data Transfer Protocol (Full Version)

▶**Proof of S2:**

First we establish the hypothesis of assertion T5, which states that an acknowledgment does not arrive before the transmitter has sent the message.

$$
\begin{aligned}
Ack(i,\delta) \;\supset\;& Ack(i,\gamma) & \text{(mrt1)} \\
\supset\;& |Y| \geq i & \text{(R2)} \\
\supset\;& M_i \in \hat{\beta} & \text{(R1)} \\
\supset\;& M_i \in \alpha & \text{(mtr1)} \\
\supset\;& |X| \geq i & \text{(T1)}
\end{aligned}
$$

This implies

$$
Ack(i,\delta) \;\supset\; |X| \geq i.
$$

We now know that the conclusion of T5 holds, so we can reason with the simpler form

$$
\forall j \left(Ack(j,\delta) \supset \left(uc(\alpha, M_{j+1}) \vee \diamond(Ack(j+1,\delta)) \right) \right). \tag{T5'}
$$

The base step of the induction is $\diamond(|Y| = 0)$, which holds initially. To prove the induction step, suppose that at some point $|Y| = k$. Let $|\beta| = j$. Then, by applying R6, either

$$
\diamond(|Y| \geq k+1), \text{ or} \tag{1}
$$

$$
\sim \diamond(\exists i \geq j \, (\beta_i = M_{k+1})) \tag{2}
$$

is true. Case (1) implies that the system proceeds. Case (2) implies that M_{k+1} never reaches the receiver. Under these circumstances, the receiver sends an unbounded number of acknowledgments for message k (R5):

$$
uc(\gamma, A_k).
$$

Commitment mrt3 guarantees that the acknowledgment arrives at the transmitter:

$$
\diamond A_k \in \delta,
$$

which implies

$$
\diamond Ack(k,\delta).
$$

T5' then implies that the $(k+1)^{st}$ message is sent an unbounded number of times,

$$
uc(\alpha, M_{k+1}), \tag{2a}
$$

or the $(k+1)^{st}$ acknowledgment is eventually received,

$$\Diamond Ack(k+1, \delta). \tag{2b}$$

Case (2a) implies $\Diamond(\exists i \geq k \, (\beta_i = M_{k+1}))$ (using mtr3). R6 then implies

$$\Diamond |Y| \geq k+1.$$

In case (2b), the system safety relations proved above show $\Diamond |Y| \geq k+1$. This completes the induction step and the proof of S2. ∎

Stenning's Protocol and the Alternating Bit Protocol

Stenning's protocol is simple to describe and works correctly with a wide variety of medium errors. One serious drawback of the protocol is that it requires sequence numbers of unbounded size, an implementation difficulty. As long as arbitrary delay and re-ordering of messages by the medium is allowed, this annoyance is necessary. As we mentioned before, Stenning [43] describes a similar protocol with cyclic sequence numbers (sequence numbers modulo some N) under the constraint that the lifetime of a message is bounded, thereby restricting the possible delay. He goes on to describe the necessary window sizes based upon the number of messages that can be transmitted per unit time and upon the maximum message lifespan.

If we constrain the medium in a different way, we can obtain another solution, that avoids unbounded sequence numbers and is only slightly more difficult to verify than the simple version presented in Section 6.5. The additional constraint would be to prohibit re-ordering of messages by the medium. This is a reasonable restriction if we are describing a communication link built upon a single wire or a single buffer. Under this restriction we find that the alternating bit protocol suffices to guarantee the safety and liveness properties we desire. The only changes to the simple version of Stenning's protocol would be that $+$ and $-$ are replaced by $\oplus$ and $\ominus$ (modulus 2) and that $<$ is replaced by $\neq$. The resulting algorithm is proved by a mixture of the techniques used for the simple version of Stenning's protocol and for the alternating bit protocol.

6.7. Brinch Hansen's Network

In the previous sections, all of the protocols have created a (virtual) reliable medium out of an unreliable medium. They guaranteed that messages would not be lost or corrupted, and that the order of the messages would be preserved. Brinch Hansen's network [7] presents a different environment, in which there are many nodes in a circular network and a number of user processes at each node. The network provides a set of virtual channels as a service to the users. The channels are fixed at the time the system is created, with each channel having exactly one sending user and one receiving user. (The users of a channel can be anywhere in the network, even at the same node.) In this network, the media between the nodes are reliable—unlike media in the previous sections, which could introduce errors or lose messages. The media are implemented by synchronized communication modules similar to those found in Hoare's communicating sequential processes [19]; a process A wishing to read from (write to) another process B using a synchronized module is delayed until B wants to write to (read from) A. See Figure 6.7–1 for a diagram of the system.

The system has $nmax$ nodes. Each node has an internal buffer with $bmax$ slots. There are $cmax$ virtual channels. To send message m using channel x, a user at node n would execute

$$n.send(x, m).$$

The corresponding action on the other end of the channel is *receive*. (These *send* and *receive* operations are implemented by operations of the *inputs* and *outputs* submodules, which are described in Section 6.7.2.)

Our first goal is to prove two safety properties of the network. The first invariant states that output from a channel is an initial subsequence of the input to that channel. The second invariant relates the length of the channel input history to the length of the channel output history: the length of the input can be at most one greater than the length of the output. We prove these properties bottom-up. Section 6.7.2 describes the safety properties of the communication medium. Section 6.7.3 presents the submodules of the nodes and the safety properties of these submodules. In Section 6.7.4, we combine the submodule invariants to form node invariants. These node invariants will entail certain assumptions concerning the operation of the entire network. In Section 6.7.5, we prove the validity of these assumptions. We prove the desired system invariants in Section 6.7.6.

Our second goal is to prove the following commitment for the network: if one user executes a *send* operation on a channel, and another user executes a

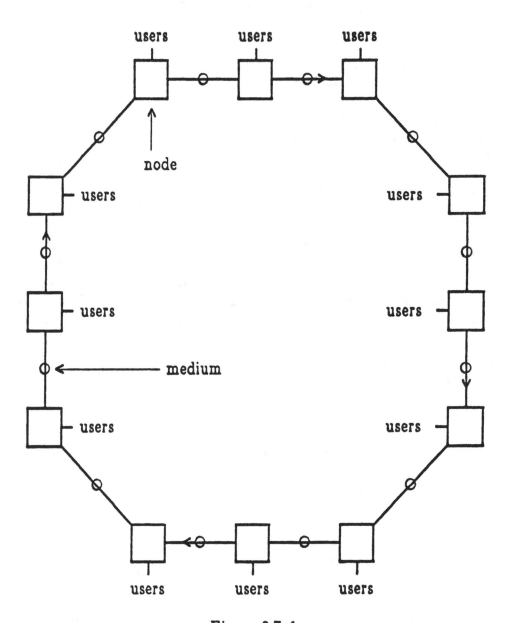

Figure 6.7-1
Brinch Hansen's Network

receive operation on that same channel, then eventually both the *send* and the *receive* operations will terminate. Section 6.7.7 discusses the liveness properties of the synchronized communication modules. Section 6.7.8 presents the liveness assertions of the submodules. In Section 6.7.9, we build node commitments out of the submodule assertions. As with the safety invariants, these node commitments contain assumptions about the operation of the entire network. In Section 6.7.10, we prove the validity of these assumptions. Section 6.7.11 contains the system liveness proof.

Brinch Hansen's network contains more hierarchical structure than the algorithms in the rest of this chapter. As a result, we shall concentrate more on how the invariants and commitments interact than on proving them from the code. The techniques of the previous sections suffice to prove all assertions in this section.

We begin our discussion of the protocol with a brief overview of the operation of Brinch Hansen's algorithm.

6.7.1. Overview

Each node of the network contains seven internal modules. A node communicates with the two media adjacent to it, its sending users, and its receiving users. Figure 6.7–2 diagrams the submodule interconnections for a single node. Each node maintains a record of the channel numbers associated with its users. A channel is an element of the *inset* of a node if the receiving user of the channel is located at that node. Similarly, a channel is an element of the *outset* of a node if the sending user of the channel is located at that node.

Each network message is a record with three fields: *kind*, *link*, and *contents*. The *kind* field has two possible values: *request* and *response*. The channel number is stored in the *link* field. The *contents* field of a *response* message contains the information to be sent. The contents field of a *request* message is empty.

Suppose that two user processes on a channel want to communicate. The sending user executes a *send* operation, and the receiving user executes a *receive*. Both users are suspended. The *receive* operation is handled by the *inputs* submodule of the receiving-user's node. The *inputs* module initiates a request to be sent to the sending-user's node at the other end of the channel. The *kind* field of the message indicates that it is a *request*, and the *link* field contains the channel number. The message is sent to the internal buffer (*buf*) of the receiving-user's node. The *writer* submodule of that node reads messages out of *buf* and sends them to the outgoing communication medium

6.7.1. Overview

(*bout*). Nodes along the way process the message as follows. The *reader* submodule reads the message from the incoming medium (*bin*). The *reader* then determines if the message is the concern of this node. If the message is a *request* destined for this node, then it is passed to the *outputs* monitor. If it is a *response* destined for this node, then it is sent to the *inputs* monitor. Messages that do not affect this node are sent to the *buf* monitor, through the *writer*, and out through *bout*. When the message reaches its destination node, it is passed by the *reader* to the *outputs* monitor. That monitor sets a flag to indicate that the sending user can proceed with its message. The sending user, if it is waiting to proceed, sends a response back into the network by way of the same *outputs* monitor. The response travels back along the network to the receiving-user's node; where it passes through the *reader* and the *inputs* monitor on its way to the receiving user. If the users are at different nodes then the pair of messages make a full circle around the network. If the users are at the same node then the messages make two circles. Further details on the operation of the node are given with the individual modules.

We shall specify the network safety properties in terms of history sequences and projections on history sequences. We shall distinguish three kinds of messages that enter a node, as specified by the following three predicates:

$$P \equiv (kind = response \quad \wedge \quad link \in inset)$$
$$Q \equiv (kind = request \quad \wedge \quad link \in outset)$$
$$R \equiv (\sim P \wedge \sim Q).$$

These three predicates are mutually exclusive, and every message belongs to one of the three categories:

$$P \supset (\sim Q \wedge \sim R)$$

$$Q \supset (\sim P \wedge \sim R)$$

$$P \vee Q \vee R.$$

Messages of type P and Q are destined for the node in question. Messages of type R belong to three subcategories, as distinguished by the predicates S, T, and U:

$$S \equiv (link \notin inset \quad \wedge \quad link \notin outset)$$
$$T \equiv (kind = response \quad \wedge \quad link \in outset)$$
$$U \equiv (kind = request \quad \wedge \quad link \in inset).$$

A message of type R must belong to exactly one of these subcategories. Messages of type S are merely "passing through" the node on their way to their

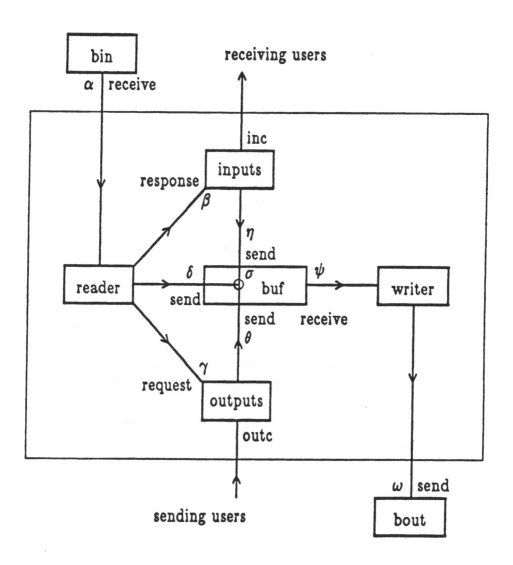

Figure 6.7-2
Node

6.7.2.   Safety: Communication Medium

destinations in other nodes. Messages of type T and U will be considered
"illegal," and in Section 6.7.5 we prove that such messages never reach a node.

In the following discussion, we often project histories on a channel number.
Such projections will be abbreviated by superscripting the history by the
channel number:

$$project(Y, link = x) \equiv Y^x.$$

6.7.2. Safety: Communication Medium

The communication medium is a black-box that represents a synchronized
communication module. Each medium has exactly one sender, called the
writer, and one receiver, called the *reader*. If the *writer* attempts to send
a message to the medium, then it will be delayed until the *reader* attempts
to receive the message. Similarly, the *reader* would be delayed if it tried to
receive a message before the *writer* had sent one. Figure 6.7-3 presents the
environment of a medium. Each medium maintains a history ω of the messages
sent to it and a history α of the messages received from it. Let z be the medium
between nodes n and $n \oplus 1$. Node n refers to z as $n.bout$. Node $n \oplus 1$ refers
to z as $(n \oplus 1).bin$.

The safety properties of the medium are specified by two invariants. The
first invariant states that nothing comes out of the medium that was not put
into the medium:

$$\alpha \preceq \omega. \tag{$M1$}$$

Because the medium is synchronized, we expect α and ω to be equal. However,
we specify *initial subsequence*, instead of *equality*, so that we can speak of node
n as having made a message available to node $n \oplus 1$ without node $n \oplus 1$ being
in the position to read that message. With the second invariant we specify that
no more than one such message can be in transit:

$$|\omega| - 1 \leq |\alpha|. \tag{$M2$}$$

The medium provides two services: send a message and receive a message.
The safety properties of these services are similar to those of the medium in
Stenning's protocol. The liveness properties, however, are different; they will
be discussed in Section 6.7.7.

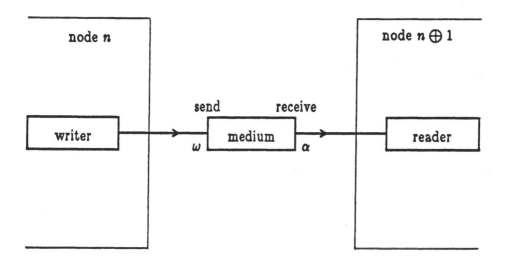

Figure 6.7–3
Medium

6.7.3.   Safety: Node Components

send(m)

  pre: $\omega = Z$
  post: $\omega = Z < m >$

receive(var m)

  pre: $\alpha = A$
  post: $\alpha = A < m >$

6.7.3. Safety: Node Components

This section describes the submodules that constitute a node. We present the code and the safety invariants for each submodule. Because our system invariants are expressed in terms of the input and output histories of a channel, we shall build our node safety assertions in terms of input/output invariants.

Reader

The *reader* separates the messages that enter the node from *bin* into three sets. The separation depends upon the relationship between the message and the node. If a message is of type *response* and the channel number is in the *inset* of the node, then the message is sent to the *inputs* module. If the message is of type *request* and the channel number is in the *outset*, then the message is sent to the *outputs* module. If the message belongs in neither category, then it is passed on to *buf*. The history of messages read from *bin* is recorded in private history α. The messages sent to *inputs*, *outputs*, and *buf* are recorded in private histories β, γ, and δ, respectively. The code for the *reader* is shown in Figure 6.7-4.

The safety properties of the *reader* are described by three invariants. They relate the predicates P, Q, and R to the histories β, γ, and δ:

$$\beta \preceq project(\alpha, P) \tag{R1}$$
$$\gamma \preceq project(\alpha, Q) \tag{R2}$$
$$\delta \preceq project(\alpha, R). \tag{R3}$$

126

```
type
    channel: 1..cmax
    message:
        record
                kind: ( request, response )
                link: channel
                contents: item
        end record


reader: process
constant
    inset, outset: set of channel
var
    m:message
begin
    loop
            bin.receive( m )
            if ( m.kind=response) and ( m.link in inset) then
                    inp.response( m )
            elseif ( m.kind=request) and ( m.link in outset) then
                    out.request( m )
            else
                    buf.send( m )
            fi
    end loop
end process
```

Figure 6.7-4
Reader

```
writer: process
var
    m:message
begin
    loop
            buf.receive( m )
            bout.send( m )
    end loop
end process
```

Figure 6.7-5
Writer

6.7.3. Safety: Node Components

Writer

The *writer* is a simplified version of the *reader*. It takes messages out of *buf* and sends them to *bout*. The *writer* is simpler than the *reader* because it has no choices to make as to where to send a message. The code for the *writer* is presented in Program 6.7-5.

The history of messages that the *writer* has read from *buf* is ψ; the history of messages that the *writer* has sent to *bout* is ω.

The *writer*'s invariant corresponds to the *reader* invariants.

$$\omega \preceq \psi \qquad\qquad (W1)$$

The Internal Buffer: Buf

The *buf* monitor is built upon a bounded fifo queue. The queue has $bmax$ slots where

$$bmax = \lceil cmax/nmax \rceil + 1.$$

This value was chosen to guarantee that if there are messages on all channels, then there is enough buffer space in the network to avoid deadlock; see Section 6.7.10 for details. We shall assume that *FifoQueue* is a predefined data type. The *put* operation adds an element onto the queue; the *get* operation removes an element from the queue. The data type includes two auxiliary functions: *empty* and *full*; initially fifo queues are empty. The *buf* monitor takes input from three sources: the *inputs* monitor, the *outputs* monitor, and the *reader*. It delivers output to *writer*. The associated history variables are η, θ, δ, and ψ. The code for *buf* can be found in Figure 6.7-6.

The names β, γ, and δ are synonyms for the components of the private input history of the buffer:

$$\delta \equiv buf.out[reader]$$
$$\eta \equiv buf.out[inputs]$$
$$\theta \equiv buf.out[outputs].$$

In addition to keeping track of the histories for each individual sender, *buf* maintains an auxiliary history σ to record all of the messages in the order that they were processed. The relationship between σ and the input histories is expressed by the invariant

$$merge(\sigma, \{\delta, \eta, \theta\}). \qquad\qquad (B1)$$

```
buf: monitor
var
        buffer: FifoQueue [bmax] of message
        σ: auxiliary history of message
        ψ, out [reader] ≡ δ, out [inputs] ≡ η,
        out [outputs] ≡ θ: private history of message
        WantToRead: auxiliary boolean

visible procedure send(m:message)
begin
        wait(not buffer.full)
        buffer.put(m)
        out [id] := out [id] Q<m>
        σ := σQ<m>
end procedure

visible procedure receive(var m:message)
begin
        WantToRead := true
        wait(not buffer.empty)
        buffer.get(m)
        ψ := ψQ<m>
        WantToRead := false
end procedure

auxiliary function full ≡ buffer.full

auxiliary function empty ≡ buffer.empty

auxiliary function WantToRead ≡ WantToRead

begin
        σ := ψ := δ := η := θ := ∅
end monitor
```

Figure 6.7-6
Buf Monitor

6.7.3. Safety: Node Components

That is, the history σ contains all of the elements of δ, η, and θ, with the relative order of the messages in the original histories preserved.

The safety properties of the *buf* monitor are described by three invariants. B1 specifies the relationship between σ and the input histories. B2 and B3 relate σ to the output history ψ:

$$\psi \preceq \sigma. \tag{B2}$$

$$|\sigma| - bmax \;\leq\; |\psi|. \tag{B3}$$

The specifications for *send* and *receive* are as follows.

send(m)

    pre: $out[id] = A$
    post: $out[id] = A < m >$

receive(var m)

    pre: $\psi = B$
    post: $\psi = B < m >$

Inputs and Outputs

The *inputs* and *outputs* monitors provide the interface between the users and the network. The *inputs* monitor is called by the *reader* submodule and by the receiving users; the *outputs* monitor is called by the *reader* submodule and by the sending users. Each of the two monitors maintains an input history of the messages received from the *reader*: β for the *inputs* monitor and γ for the *outputs* monitor. Both monitors send their output to *buf*; the associated output histories are η for the *inputs* monitor and θ for the *outputs* monitor. Both monitors are called by users, and they each have histories associated with each channel: $inc[x]$ for the *inputs* monitor and $outc[x]$ for the *outputs* monitor. Figures 6.7-7 and 6.7-8 present the code of the two monitors.

In the *outputs* monitor, requests that have been received, but not yet processed, are recorded in the *ready* array. In the *inputs* monitor, the *hold* array stores the contents of responses until the information is passed to the receiving users.

inputs: monitor
var

      hold: **array** [*channel*] of *message*
      β, *inc* [*channel*] : private *history* of *message*

visible procedure *receive* (*x:channel;* **var** *v:item*)
var   *m:message*
begin

      m.kind := *request*
      m.link := *x*
      buf.send(*m*)
      wait (*hold* [*x*] $\neq$ *empty*)
      v := *hold* [*x*] .*contents*
      inc [*x*] := *inc* [*x*] @<*v*>
      hold [*x*] := *empty*
end procedure

visible procedure *response* (*m:message*)
begin

      hold [*m.link*] := *m*
      β := β@<*m*>
end procedure

begin

      β := $\emptyset$
      $\forall$ *z* (*inc* [*z*] := $\emptyset$)
      $\forall$ *z* (*hold* [*z*] := *empty*)
end monitor

Figure 6.7–7
Inputs Monitor

outputs: monitor
var

      ready: array [*channel*] of *boolean*

      γ, outc [*channel*] : private *history* of *message*

visible procedure *send* (*x:channel; v:item*)
var   *m: message*
begin

      wait (*ready* [*x*])

      m.kind := *response*

      m.link := *x*

      m.contents := *v*

      outc [*x*] := *outc* [*x*] @<*v*>

      ready [*x*] := *false*

      buf.send (*m*)

end procedure

visible procedure *request* (*m:message*)
begin

      ready [*m.link*] := *true*

      γ := γ@<*m*>

end procedure

begin

      γ := $\emptyset$

      $\forall$ *x* (*outc* [*x*] := $\emptyset$)

      $\forall$ *x* (*ready* [*x*] := *false*)

end monitor

Figure 6.7–8
Outputs Monitor

6.7.3. Safety: Node Components

All invariants of the *inputs* and *outputs* monitors involve projections on a channel. The first pair of assertions compare the number of messages that have been sent on a channel to the number that have been received from that channel. The *inputs* monitor can send at most one more message than it has received:

$$\forall x \, (|\eta^x| - 1 \;\leq\; |\beta^x| \;\leq\; |\eta^x|). \qquad (I1)$$

The *outputs* monitor can never send more messages than it has received:

$$\forall x \, (|\gamma^x| - 1 \;\leq\; |\theta^x| \;\leq\; |\gamma^x|). \qquad (O1)$$

The next two invariants relate the user histories *inc* and *outc* to β and θ:

$$\forall x \, (inc[x] \preceq \beta^x.contents) \qquad (I2)$$

$$\forall x \, (\theta^x.contents \preceq outc[x]) \qquad (O2)$$

The notation $Y.field$, where Y is a history variable and *field* is a component of the messages in Y, is interpreted as the history

$$< Y_i.field >_{i=1}^{|Y|} \, .$$

Invariants I3 and O3 relate the lengths of η^x and γ^x to the lengths of $inc[x]$ and $outc[x]$:

$$\forall x \, (|\eta^x| \;\leq\; |inc[x]| + 1) \qquad (I3)$$

$$\forall x \, (|outc[x]| \;\leq\; |\gamma^x|). \qquad (O3)$$

The fourth pair of invariants describes the type of messages that the *inputs* and *outputs* monitors insert into the network:

$$\forall x \, \big(\forall m \in \eta^x \, (x \in inset \;\;\wedge\;\; m.kind = request)\big) \qquad (I4)$$

$$\forall x \, \big(\forall m \in \theta^x \, (x \in outset \;\;\wedge\;\; m.kind = response)\big). \qquad (O4)$$

The final invariant specifies the lengths of η and *inc*, when a receiving user is about to execute a *receive* operation:

$$at \; inputs.receive(x, v) \;\;\supset\;\; |\eta^x| = |inc[x]|. \qquad (I5)$$

Each monitor provides two services: one for the user and one for the *reader*. Users call *inputs.receive(x, m)* to receive a message from channel x, and they call *outputs.send(x, m)* to send message m on a channel x. The *reader* calls the *inputs.response* procedure to pass along a message of type *response* from the network; it calls the *outputs.request* procedure to pass along a message of type *request*.

Services of the *inputs* monitor:

6.7.4. Safety: Node

receive(x; var v)

   pre: $inc[x] = A$
   post: $inc[x] = A < v >$

response(m)

   pre: $\beta = B$
   post: $\beta = B < m >$

Services of the *outputs* monitor:

send(x,v)

   pre: $outc[x] = A$
   post: $outc[x] = A < v >$

request(m)

   pre: $\gamma = B$
   post: $\gamma = B < m >$

6.7.4. Safety: Node

The previous section described the safety properties of the submodules that constitute a node. In this section we combine the submodule invariants to specify the safety properties of the node as whole. The system invariant that we eventually want to prove is that the output from a channel is an initial subsequence of the input to that channel. (We also want to relate the length of the input history to the length of the output history.) We shall select node invariants towards this end; the invariants will specify the output of each node with respect to its input. Depending on the relationship between a channel and the node, the output history can be *inc* or ω, and the input history can be *outc* or α.

A node can interact with a channel in one of four ways: the channel is in neither the *inset* nor the *outset* of the node, the channel is in the *inset* but not the *outset* of the node, the channel is in the *outset* but not the *inset* of the node, or the channel is in both the *inset* and the *outset* of the node. We first prove five assertions that are used in considering these four cases. We then analyze each case in turn to derive its input/output relationship.

Independent of the node/channel relationship, the output ω of the node is an initial subsequence of the input σ to the internal buffer. Invariants W1 and B2 imply

$$\omega \preceq \psi \preceq \sigma. \tag{1}$$

6.7.4. Safety: Node

Assertions (2) and (3) involve the *inputs* monitor. Invariant R1 states that

$$\beta \preceq project(\alpha, P).$$

We project R1 on the channel number to obtain

$$\forall x \left(\beta^x \preceq project(\alpha, P)^x\right).$$

If x is not in the *inset*, then the definition of P implies that no messages of that channel are sent to the *inputs* monitor:

$$\forall x \notin inset \left(project(\alpha, P)^x = \emptyset\right). \tag{2}$$

Similarly, invariant I4 implies

$$\forall x \notin inset \left(\eta^x = \emptyset\right). \tag{3}$$

Similar reasoning for the *outputs* monitor allows us to conclude

$$\forall x \notin outset \left(project(\alpha, Q)^x = \emptyset\right) \tag{4}$$

and

$$\forall x \notin outset \left(\theta^x = \emptyset\right). \tag{5}$$

Figure 6.7–9 summarizes the submodule invariants and the five assertions we have just proved.

We shall now consider the four ways in which a node and a channel can interact. For the remainder of Section 6.7.4, all histories will be projected on channel x; therefore, the superscript will not be written. Similarly, the histories *inc* and *outc* will have an implicit index of x.

In the first case the channel and the node are unrelated; suppose that $x \notin inset \wedge x \notin outset$. Assertions (2) and (3) imply that $project(\alpha, P) = \emptyset$ and $project(\alpha, Q) = \emptyset$. For every message, one predicate of P, Q, or R must be true; therefore, we can conclude that $project(\alpha, R) = \alpha$. Invariant R3 then implies

$$\delta \preceq \alpha. \tag{6}$$

Assertions (3) and (5) imply that the node does not contribute messages to channel x: $\eta = \theta = \emptyset$. Invariant B1 therefore implies

$$\sigma = \delta. \tag{7}$$

We can combine (1), (6), and (7) to conclude

$$x \notin inset \wedge x \notin outset \quad \supset \quad \omega \preceq \alpha. \tag{N1}$$

$$\alpha \preceq \omega \tag{M1}$$

$$|\omega| - 1 \leq |\alpha| \tag{M2}$$

$$\beta \preceq project(\alpha, P) \tag{R1}$$

$$\gamma \preceq project(\alpha, Q) \tag{R2}$$

$$\delta \preceq project(\alpha, R) \tag{R3}$$

$$\omega \preceq \psi \tag{W1}$$

$$merge(\sigma, \{\delta, \eta, \theta\}) \tag{B1}$$

$$\psi \preceq \sigma \tag{B2}$$

$$|\sigma| - bmax \leq |\psi| \tag{B3}$$

$$\forall z \left(|\eta^z| - 1 \leq |\beta^z| \leq |\eta^z|\right) \tag{I1}$$

$$\forall z \left(inc[z] \preceq \beta^z.contents\right) \tag{I2}$$

$$\forall z \left(|\eta^z| \leq |inc[z]| + 1\right) \tag{I3}$$

$$\forall z \left(\forall m \in \eta^z \left(z \in inset \land m.kind = request\right)\right) \tag{I4}$$

$$at\ inputs.receive(z, v) \supset |\eta^z| = |inc[z]| \tag{I5}$$

$$\forall z \left(|\gamma^z| - 1 \leq |\theta^z| \leq |\gamma^z|\right) \tag{O1}$$

$$\forall z \left(\theta^z.contents \preceq outc[z]\right) \tag{O2}$$

$$\forall z \left(|outc[z]| \leq |\gamma^z|\right) \tag{O3}$$

$$\forall z \left(\forall m \in \theta^z \left(z \in outset \land m.kind = response\right)\right) \tag{O4}$$

$$\omega \preceq \psi \preceq \sigma \tag{1}$$

$$\forall z \notin inset \left(project(\alpha, P)^z = \emptyset\right) \tag{2}$$

$$\forall z \notin inset \left(\eta^z = \emptyset\right) \tag{3}$$

$$\forall z \notin outset \left(project(\alpha, Q)^z = \emptyset\right) \tag{4}$$

$$\forall z \notin outset \left(\theta^z = \emptyset\right) \tag{5}$$

Figure 6.7-9
Table of Submodule Invariants

6.7.4. Safety: Node

In the second case, the node is partially related to the channel. Suppose that x is in the *inset* of the node, but not in the *outset*: $x \in inset \land x \notin outset$. Invariant R1 states that $\beta \preceq project(\alpha, P)$; invariant I2 states that $inc \preceq \beta.contents$. We can, therefore, conclude that

$$x \in inset \land x \notin outset \quad \supset \quad inc \preceq project(\alpha, P).contents. \qquad (8)$$

Assertion (4) states that $project(\alpha, Q) = \emptyset$. The messages that are not in categories P or Q must be in category R. A message of type R must belong to exactly one of the subcategories S, T, or U. The assumption that $x \in inset$ implies that predicate S is false. The assumption that $x \notin outset$ implies that predicate T is false. Therefore, all messages of type R must be of type U:

$$project(\alpha, R) = project(\alpha, U). \qquad (9)$$

As a result, R3 implies

$$\delta \preceq project(\alpha, U). \qquad (10)$$

At this point we identify the messages of type U as "illegal." Such messages have $kind = request$ and $link \in inset$. But these are the messages that this node sends out! This node serves the receiving user but not the sending user. Requests are sent from this node to the sending user's node. That node should absorb these requests and issue responses. Therefore, if the system is working correctly, this node (under the current assumptions) should not receive its own requests. We take the correct operation of the system as an assumption to be proved later. Assertions (4), (9), and (10) allow us to conclude that

$$project(\alpha, U) = \emptyset \quad \supset \quad \delta = \emptyset \land \alpha = project(\alpha, P). \qquad (11)$$

We can, therefore, simplify the conclusion of assertion (8) and obtain

$$x \in inset \land x \notin outset \land project(\alpha, U) = \emptyset \quad \supset \quad inc \preceq \alpha.contents. \qquad (N2)$$

Invariant B1 and assertions (1), (5), and (11) imply

$$project(\alpha, U) = \emptyset \quad \supset \quad \omega \preceq \eta. \qquad (12)$$

Invariant I4 states that all of the elements of η are requests on channel x; therefore, the messages are identical. We need only keep track of the number of requests. Combining assertion (12) and invariant I3, we can relate ω to inc:

$$x \in inset \land x \notin outset \land project(\alpha, U) = \emptyset \quad \supset \quad |\omega| \leq |inc| + 1. \qquad (N3)$$

We can combine assertion (12) and invariant I4 in a different way to yield:

$$x \in inset \land x \notin outset \land project(\alpha, U) = \emptyset \quad \supset \\ \forall m \in \omega \, (m.kind = request \land m.link = x). \qquad (N4)$$

6.7.4. Safety: Node

The third case, $z \in outset \wedge z \notin inset$, is similar to the second case, and through similar reasoning we conclude

$$z \in outset \wedge z \notin inset \wedge project(\alpha, T) = \emptyset \quad \supset \quad w.contents \preceq outc, \quad (N5)$$

$$z \in outset \wedge z \notin inset \wedge project(\alpha, T) = \emptyset \quad \supset \quad |outc| \leq |\alpha|, \quad (N6)$$

and

$$z \in outset \wedge z \notin inset \wedge project(\alpha, T) = \emptyset \quad \supset \\ \forall m \in \omega \; (m.kind = response \wedge m.link = z). \quad (N7)$$

The final case occurs when the node serves both the sending user and the receiving user of the channel: $z \in inset \wedge z \in outset$. Assertions (2) through (5) do not simplify this situation because both requests and responses on channel z enter the node on α and leave the node on ω. The reasoning, however, is similar to the previous two cases; the resulting conclusions are

$$z \in inset \wedge z \in outset \quad \supset \\ project(\omega, kind = response).contents \quad \preceq \quad outc \quad (N8)$$

$$z \in inset \wedge z \in outset \quad \supset \\ inc \quad \preceq \quad project(\alpha, kind = response).contents \quad (N9)$$

$$z \in inset \wedge z \in outset \quad \supset \\ |outc| \quad \leq \quad |project(\alpha, kind = request)| \quad (N10)$$

$$z \in inset \wedge z \in outset \quad \supset \\ |project(\omega, kind = request)| \quad \leq \quad |inc| + 1. \quad (N11)$$

In the Section 6.7.11, we shall discuss the values of inc and $outc$ when a receiving user is at $receive$. Using the same techniques as above we combine I5 and (12) to show

$$z \in inset \wedge z \notin outset \wedge project(\alpha, U) = \emptyset \wedge \text{at } receive(z, v) \quad \supset \\ |\omega| \leq |inc|. \quad (N12)$$

Similarly, we can show

$$z \in inset \wedge z \in outset \wedge \text{at } receive(z, v) \quad \supset \\ |project(\omega, kind = request)| \quad \leq \quad |inc|. \quad (N13)$$

6.7.5. *Safety: The Relationship Between the Nodes*

Outstanding Messages

In the Section 6.7.10, we shall want to know how many messages may be outstanding on a given channel. New messages are created only by the *inputs* and *outputs* monitors of a node. Similarly, those two monitors are the only ones that can consume old messages. (All other components of the node merely pass messages along.) Therefore, we define $outstanding(n, x)$, meaning the number of message originated by node n minus the number consumed by node n, to be

$$outstanding(n, x) = (|\eta^x| - |\beta^x|) + (|\theta^x| - |\gamma^x|).$$

Note that if x is not in the *inset* of n, then the first term equals 0. Similarly, if x is not in the *outset* of n, then the second term equals 0. Invariants I1 and O1 then imply

$$x \in n.inset \supset outstanding(n, x) \leq 1 \qquad (N14)$$

$$x \notin n.inset \supset outstanding(n, x) \leq 0. \qquad (N15)$$

6.7.5. Safety: The Relationship Between the Nodes

In the last section, we derived fifteen invariants that described the safety specifications of a node. Six of these node invariants contained assumptions about the correct behavior of the system, implying that no "illegal" messages are received. In this section we prove that these assumptions are valid.

Communication from node A to node B requires sending a request from B to A and then a response from A to B. To describe the position of a message with respect to its source and destination, we need to define when one node is between two other nodes. Let the nodes be numbered 0 to $nmax - 1$. Consider $\oplus$ to be addition modulo $nmax$ and $\ominus$ to be subtraction modulo $nmax$. We define $between(y; a, b)$, meaning that node y is between nodes a and b, to be

$$between(y; a, b) \quad \equiv \quad y \neq a \wedge y \neq b \wedge ((b \ominus y) + (y \ominus a) = b \ominus a).$$

The definition of *between** states that y is neither a nor b, and if we follow the network in a clockwise direction from a to y and continue clockwise from y to b, we pass by as many nodes as if we had gone clockwise from a to b.

---

*I would like to thank David Wall for this formulation of *between*.

6.7.5. Safety: The Relationship Between the Nodes

We have assumed that each channel has exactly one sender and exactly one receiver. We state this assumption as

$$\forall z \in channel \left(\exists! \, n \in node \left(n = sender(z) \right) \right)$$
$$\forall z \in channel \left(\exists! \, n \in node \left(n = receiver(z) \right) \right),$$

where $channel = 1 \ldots cmaz$, $node = 0 \ldots nmaz - 1$, and $sender$ and $receiver$ are defined as follows:

$$n = sender(z) \quad \equiv \quad z \in n.outset$$
$$n = receiver(z) \quad \equiv \quad z \in n.inset.$$

We want to prove that requests on a channel remain between the $receiver$ and the $sender$ of that channel and that responses on a channel remain between the $sender$ and $receiver$. To state this property we define under what conditions it is proper for a node to receive a message and for a node to send a message. Let $z = m.link$; we define $proper\text{-}to\text{-}receive_n(m)$, meaning that message m is proper to receive at node n, as

$$proper\text{-}to\text{-}receive_n(m) =$$
$$\left(m.kind = request \quad \supset \right.$$
$$n = sender(z) \quad \lor \quad between(n; receiver(z), sender(z))) \quad \land$$
$$\left(m.kind = response \quad \supset \right.$$
$$n = receiver(z) \quad \lor \quad between(n; sender(z), receiver(z))).$$

Similarly, we define $proper\text{-}to\text{-}send_n(m)$, meaning that a message m is proper to send from a node n, as

$$proper\text{-}to\text{-}send_n(m) =$$
$$\left(m.kind = request \quad \supset \right.$$
$$n = receiver(z) \quad \lor \quad between(n; receiver(z), sender(z))) \quad \land$$
$$\left(m.kind = response \quad \supset \right.$$
$$n = sender(z) \quad \lor \quad between(n; sender(z), receiver(z))).$$

To insure that messages remain in the correct set of nodes, we prove that if a node never receives improper messages, then it only sends proper messages, that is, for every node n

$$\forall p \in \alpha \left(proper\text{-}to\text{-}receive_n(p) \right) \quad \supset \quad \forall q \in \omega \left(proper\text{-}to\text{-}send_n(q) \right). \quad (1)$$

To prove (1) we project the input and output histories of the node n on an arbitrary channel z. We then show that each combination of channel and node satisfies (1). As in the previous section, there are four cases to be considered. For the remainder of Section 6.7.5, all histories will be projected on channel z, and the superscripts will not be written.

6.7.5. Safety: The Relationship Between the Nodes

▶**Proof of** (1):

In each case we shall assume that all messages of α are *proper-to-receive*. We shall then show that all messages of ω are *proper-to-send*.

In the first case, n is neither the *sender* nor the *receiver* of x. Invariant N1 implies that $\omega \preceq \alpha$. Therefore, node n contributes no new messages to ω. We assume that all the messages of α are *proper-to-receive*. Because n is neither the *sender* nor the *receiver*, the definition of *proper-to-send* and *proper-to-receive* are the same. Hence, all messages of ω are *proper-to-send*.

In the second case, we have $n = receiver(x) \wedge n \neq sender(x)$. In the last section we proved that in this situation $project(\alpha, R) = project(\alpha, U)$. A message m is of type U (at node n), if m is a request and n is the *receiver* of $m.link$; such a message is not *proper-to-receive*. Therefore, if all messages are *proper-to-receive*, then $project(\alpha, U) = \emptyset$. Invariant N4 then implies that

$$\forall m \in \omega \, (m.kind = request \wedge n = receiver(m.link)),$$

which implies that all messages in ω are *proper-to-send*.

The third case, $n = sender(x) \wedge n \neq receiver(x)$, is similar to the second case. Instead of showing that $project(\alpha, U) = \emptyset$, we show that $project(\alpha, T) = \emptyset$.

For the final case, $n = sender(x) \wedge n = receiver(x)$, it is trivally true that all messages in ω are *proper-to-send*. Because n is both the *sender* and the *receiver*, it is the *sender* for all *response* messages and the *receiver* for all *request* messages. The definition of *proper-to-send* is true in both of these situations. ∎

Now we show that a message that was proper for node n to send is proper for node $n \oplus 1$ to receive:

$$
\begin{aligned}
\forall p \in n.\omega \, \big(proper\text{-}to\text{-}send_n(p)\big) \quad &\supset \\
\forall q \in (n \oplus 1).\alpha \, &\big(proper\text{-}to\text{-}receive_{n \oplus 1}(q)\big).
\end{aligned}
\tag{2}
$$

6.7.5. Safety: The Relationship Between the Nodes

▶**Proof of** (2):

For a *request* message m to be *proper-to-send$_n$*, it must be the case that $n = receiver(m.link)$ or $between(n; receiver(m.link), sender(m.link))$. If n is the *receiver*, then either $n \oplus 1$ is between the *receiver* and the *sender*, or $n \oplus 1$ is the *sender*. In either case m is *proper-to-receive*. If n is between the *receiver* and the *sender*, then either $n \oplus 1$ is also between, or $n \oplus 1$ is the *sender*. Again, for both of these cases m is *proper-to-receive*. The proof for a *response* message is similar. ∎

Improper Messages

We must now discuss the behavior of a node if it receives a message that is not *proper-to-receive*. We approach the problem by determining how the *reader* submodule reacts to such a message. We then extend that result to a node assertion.

The *reader* submodule possesses a fourth invariant that describes its response to improper messages. The *reader* of node n must read in an improper message before it can pass an improper message to the buffer (and when it reads the first such message, it has not yet sent any such messages):

$$at\ init \wedge \diamond(\exists\, m \in \alpha\,(\sim proper\text{-}to\text{-}receive_n(m)))\quad \supset$$
$$\diamond(\exists\, m \in \alpha\,(\sim proper\text{-}to\text{-}receive_n(m)) \wedge \forall\, m' \in \delta\,(proper\text{-}to\text{-}send_n(m'))),$$
$$(R4)$$

where *init* refers to the initialization of the *reader*. We did not present this invariant in Section 6.7.3, because at that point we had not defined *proper-to-send* and *proper-to-receive*.

Extending R4 to the node level, we note that invariants I4 and O4 imply that η and θ contribute no messages to σ that are improper to send. The *writer* merely passes the messages to *bout*. Therefore, the node invariant is

$$at\ n.init \wedge \diamond(\exists\, m \in n.\alpha\,(\sim proper\text{-}to\text{-}receive_n(m)))\quad \supset$$
$$\diamond(\exists\, m \in n.\alpha\,(\sim proper\text{-}to\text{-}receive_n(m))\ \wedge$$
$$\forall\, m' \in n.\omega\,(proper\text{-}to\text{-}send_n(m'))).$$
$$(N16)$$

6.7.6. Safety: System

Proper Messages

We now know that if all of the messages received by a node are *proper-to-receive*, then that node will only send messages that are *proper-to-send*. Furthermore, these messages that are sent will be proper for the next node to receive. We want to prove that all messages received by a node are *proper-to-receive*:

$$\forall m \in n.\alpha\big(\text{proper-to-receive}_n(m)\big). \qquad (RBN1)$$

▶**Proof of** RBN1:

Initially all of the α histories are empty, and (trivially) all messages in these histories are *proper-to-receive*.

Suppose that n receives an improper message. Invariant N16 implies that when the first such message is received, no improper messages have been sent by n. Using the contrapositive of assertion (2), we can conclude that $n \ominus 1$ has sent an improper message. But, by the contrapositive of (1), $n \ominus 1$ had received an improper message. We carry this reasoning around the cycle of nodes until we deduce that $n \oplus 1$ must have received an improper message from n. That is a contradiction; therefore, n can never receive an improper message. ■

6.7.6. Safety: System

In Section 6.7.4, we proved a set of invariants that described the safety properties of the individual nodes. The node invariants are summarized in Figure 6.7–10. In Section 6.7.5, we showed that the nodes always received proper messages. In this section, we combine the results of the previous two sections in order to derive the system invariants:

$$\forall x \, (receiver(x).inc[x] \preceq sender(x).outc[x]) \qquad (S1)$$

$$\forall x \, (|sender(x).outc[x]| \ \leq \ |receiver(x).inc[x]| + 1). \qquad (S2)$$

We first show that RBN1 implies that

$$x \in n.inset \wedge x \notin n.outset \quad \supset \quad project(n.\alpha^x, U) = \emptyset \qquad (1)$$

$$x \in n.outset \wedge x \notin n.inset \quad \supset \quad project(n.\alpha^x, T) = \emptyset. \qquad (2)$$

Proving (1) and (2) will simplify the node assertions.

$$x \notin inset \wedge x \notin outset \quad \supset \quad \omega \preceq \alpha \tag{N1}$$

$$x \in inset \wedge x \notin outset \wedge project(\alpha, U) = \emptyset \quad \supset \quad inc \preceq \alpha.contents \tag{N2}$$

$$x \in inset \wedge x \notin outset \wedge project(\alpha, U) = \emptyset \quad \supset \quad |\omega| \leq |inc| + 1 \tag{N3}$$

$$x \in outset \wedge x \notin inset \wedge project(\alpha, T) = \emptyset \quad \supset \quad \omega.contents \preceq outc, \tag{N5}$$

$$x \in outset \wedge x \notin inset \wedge project(\alpha, T) = \emptyset \quad \supset \quad |outc| \leq |\alpha|, \tag{N6}$$

$$x \in inset \wedge x \in outset \quad \supset \quad project(\omega, kind = response).contents \preceq outc \tag{N8}$$

$$x \in inset \wedge x \in outset \quad \supset \quad inc \preceq project(\alpha, kind = response).contents \tag{N9}$$

$$x \in inset \wedge x \in outset \quad \supset \quad |outc| \leq |project(\alpha, kind = request)| \tag{N10}$$

$$x \in inset \wedge x \in outset \quad \supset \quad |project(\omega, kind = request)| \leq |inc| + 1 \tag{N11}$$

N4 and N7 will not be used again in this section.
N12 and N13 are used in Section 6.7.11.
N14 and N15 are used in Section 6.7.10.

Figure 6.7–10
Table of Node Invariants

6.7.6. Safety: System

▶**Proof of** (1):

If we assume that $x \in n.inset \land x \notin n.outset$, then $n = receiver(x)$ and $n \neq sender(x)$. The definition of U implies that

$$\forall m \in project(n.\alpha^x, U)\,(m.kind = request \land m.link = x).$$

Assertion RBN1 implies that for every node n

$$\forall m \in \alpha\,(proper\text{-}to\text{-}receive_n(m)),$$

The definition of *proper-to-receive* states that if m is a request on x, then n must either be $sender(x)$, or be between $sender(x)$ and $receiver(x)$. Because n satisfies neither criteria, it can not receive requests on x. Therefore, we can deduce that

$$project(\alpha^x, U) = \emptyset. \qquad \blacksquare$$

The proof of (2) is similar. For the remainder of Section 6.7.6 we shall project all histories on x and not include the superscripts.

▶**Proof of** (S1):

- If $sender(x) \neq receiver(x)$, then invariant N2 implies that

$$receiver(x).inc[x] \preceq receiver(x).\alpha.contents. \tag{3}$$

For each intermediate node n between $sender(x)$ and $receiver(x)$, invariants N1 and M1 imply

$$(n \oplus 1).\alpha \preceq n.\alpha. \tag{4}$$

For the node immediately after the *sender*, invariant M1 implies

$$(sender(x) \oplus 1).\alpha \preceq sender(x).\omega. \tag{5}$$

Finally, invariant N5 implies

$$sender(x).\omega.contents \preceq sender(x).outc[x]. \tag{6}$$

Combining assertions (3), (4), (5), and (6) we obtain

$$receiver(x).inc[x] \preceq sender(x).outc[x].$$

6.7.6. Safety: System

- If $sender(x) = receiver(x) = k$, then invariant N9 implies

$$k.inc[x] \preceq project(k.\alpha, kind = response).contents. \qquad (7)$$

For every other node $n \neq k$, invariants N1 and M1 imply

$$(n \oplus 1).\alpha \preceq n.\alpha. \qquad (8)$$

For node $k \oplus 1$, invariant M1 implies

$$(k \oplus 1).\alpha \preceq k.\omega. \qquad (9)$$

Following the network around to node k, invariant N8 implies

$$project(k.\omega, kind = response).contents \preceq k.outc[x]. \qquad (10)$$

From assertions (7), (8), (9), and (10) we can conclude

$$receiver(x).inc[x] \preceq sender(x).outc[x]. \qquad \blacksquare$$

We prove S2 in the same way.

▶**Proof of S2 (outline):**

We discuss only the case for $sender(x) \neq receiver(x)$. The case when they are equal is similar. Assertion N6 implies that

$$|sender(x).outc[x]| \leq |sender(x).\alpha^x|.$$

Using N1 and M1 for the intermediate nodes, we can show

$$sender(x).\alpha^x \preceq receiver(x).\omega^x,$$

which implies

$$|sender(x).\alpha^x| \leq |receiver(x).\omega^x|.$$

Finally N3 implies

$$|receiver(x).\omega^x| \leq |receiver(c).inc[x]| + 1,$$

from which we can conclude S2. ■

6.7.7. Liveness: Communication Medium

The safety properties of the communication medium are the same as those of a single element buffer: the output looks like the input, but the output can have one less element. The liveness properties, however, are different. If a *send* operation is executed on a single element buffer, and if that buffer is empty, then the *send* operation will terminate; the sender can proceed, even if the receiver never receives the message. The receiver, however, always waits for the sender to send a message before it can proceed. In a synchronized communication module, the liveness properties of *send* and *receive* are symmetric: each party must wait until the other executes the corresponding operation.

In Section 6.7.2, we described the two services of the medium: *send* and *receive*. We now add two auxiliary functions to describe the synchronized nature of the medium: *TryingToReceive* and *TryingToSend*. Our view of the medium's operation is as follows. The *reader* executes a *receive* operation and sets *TryingToReceive* equal to true; the *reader* then waits. Either before, during, or after this action by the *reader*, the *writer* executes a *send* operation and sets *TryingToSend* equal to true; the writer then waits. The module then transfers the data, resets the auxiliary functions to false, and permits both the *send* and *receive* operations to terminate. We make only one synchronization assumption for the sake of the proof: there exists a time after both the *send* and *receive* operations have started when *TryingToReceive* and *TryingToSend* are both true. The formal service specifications are as follows.

send(m)

    live: $\Diamond(\textit{TryingToSend})$ $\wedge$ $(\Diamond(\textit{TryingToReceive}) \supset \Diamond(\textit{after send}))$

receive(var m)

    live: $\Diamond(\textit{TryingToReceive})$ $\wedge$ $(\Diamond(\textit{TryingToSend}) \supset \Diamond(\textit{after receive}))$

We assume in these service specifications that there is exactly one sending process (*writer* of the previous node) and exactly one receiving process (*reader* of the next node). These assumptions are stated as

$$\sim \textit{TryingToReceive} \wedge \Box(\sim \textit{reader at receive}) \quad \supset \quad \Box(\sim \textit{TryingToReceive})$$
$$\sim \textit{TryingToSend} \wedge \Box(\sim \textit{writer at send}) \quad \supset \quad \Box(\sim \textit{TryingToSend}).$$

We also specify invariants that describe the input and output histories if either process becomes blocked. In Section 6.7.2, we stated that the *writer* records its output in ω even if the *reader* never executes its *receive* operation. The next

6.7.8. *Liveness: Node Components*

two invariants embody that statement:

$$\text{writer at } send(m) \wedge \omega = Z \wedge \square(\sim TryingToReceive) \quad \supset$$
$$\diamond\square(\omega = Z < m > \quad \wedge \quad TryingToSend) \tag{ML1}$$
$$\text{reader at } receive \wedge \alpha = A \wedge \square(\sim TryingToSend) \quad \supset$$
$$\diamond\square(\alpha = A \quad \wedge \quad TryingToReceive). \tag{ML2}$$

From the liveness specification above, we can derive a commitment that we shall use in the system liveness proof:

$$c(\omega, m) = k \wedge \diamond(TryingToReceive) \supset \diamond\big(c(\alpha, m) = k\big). \tag{ML3}$$

In other words, if the *writer* has sent k copies of message m to the medium, and the *reader* is infinitely often ready to receive a message, then eventually message m will be received k times. For the remainder of Section 6.7, we shall consider two messages to be equal if they have the same *link* and *kind* fields.

6.7.8. Liveness: Node Components

In this section, we describe the liveness properties of the node submodules. Our goal is to prove the system liveness property: if users *send* and *receive* on the same channel, then the *send* and *receive* operations eventually terminate. To prove this property, we shall show that requests eventually reach the *sender* of the channel and that responses eventually reach the *receiver* of the channel. Keeping this goal in mind, we state our submodule liveness properties in terms of messages eventually being transferred from input histories to output histories.

Reader

We specify the liveness properties of the *reader* by four commitments. The first asserts that the receiver can be blocked only by the *buf.send* operation and by the *bin.receive* operation. The liveness properties of *inputs.response* and *outputs.request* are stated later in this section; both operations unconditionally terminate. The first invariant is

$$\square\diamond(\sim buf.full) \supset \square\diamond(bin.TryingToReceive). \tag{RL1}$$

6.7.8. Liveness: Node Components

▶**Proof of** RL1:

If we assume that $\square\diamond(\sim buf.full)$, then the only statement at which the *reader* can block is *bin.receive*. Therefore, we can state that $\square\diamond(at\ bin.receive)$. If the *reader* is ever perpetually blocked at *bin.receive*, then commitment ML2 implies

$$\diamond\square(TryingToReceive).$$

On the other hand, if *bin.receive* always terminates then the live-assertion of *bin.receive* implies

$$\square\diamond(TryingToReceive). \qquad \blacksquare$$

The other three commitments describe the actions of the *reader* with respect to the different types of messages it can receive. If the reader is located at node n, then it will pass requests and responses for n to the *outputs* and *inputs* monitors, and it will send other messages to *buf*:

$$
\begin{aligned}
&\big(c(\alpha,m)=k\ \wedge \\
&\quad receiver(m.link)=n\wedge m.kind=response\big)\ \supset \\
&\qquad \diamond\big(c(\beta,m)=k\big)
\end{aligned}
\qquad (RL2)
$$

$$
\begin{aligned}
&\big(c(\alpha,m)=k\ \wedge \\
&\quad sender(m.link)=n\wedge m.kind=request\big)\ \supset \\
&\qquad \diamond\big(c(\gamma,m)=k\big)
\end{aligned}
\qquad (RL3)
$$

$$
\begin{aligned}
&\big(c(\alpha,m)=k\wedge\square\diamond(\sim buf.full)\wedge \\
&\quad sender(m.link)\neq n\wedge receiver(m.link)\neq n\big)\ \supset \\
&\qquad \diamond\big(c(\delta,m)=k\big).
\end{aligned}
\qquad (RL4)
$$

Writer

The *writer* commitments are similar to the *reader* commitments:

$$\square\diamond(bout.TryingToReceive)\ \supset\ \square\diamond(buf.WantToRead) \qquad (WL1)$$

$$c(\psi,m)=k\wedge\square\diamond(bout.TryingToReceive)\ \supset\ \diamond\big(c(\omega,m)=k\big). \qquad (WL2)$$

The term *WantToRead* is an auxiliary function of the *buf* monitor; it is similar to the *TryingToReceive* function of the *bin* module.

6.7.8. Liveness: Node Components

Buf

In addition to the two services described in Section 6.7.3, the *buf* monitor provides two auxiliary functions: *full* and *empty*. The first pair of invariants relates the values of *empty* and *full* to the input and output histories of *buf*:

$$buf.empty \quad \equiv \quad (|\psi| = |\sigma|) \qquad (BL1)$$
$$buf.full \quad \equiv \quad (|\psi| + bmax = |\sigma|). \qquad (BL2)$$

The next three invariants specify the relationship between the input histories and the merged history σ. All three invariants are implied by invariant B1:

$$receiver(m.link) = n \wedge m.kind = request \quad \supset \quad c(\eta, m) = c(\sigma, m) \quad (BL3)$$
$$sender(m.link) = n \wedge m.kind = response \quad \supset \quad c(\theta, m) = c(\sigma, m) \quad (BL4)$$
$$sender(m.link) \neq n \wedge receiver(m.link) \neq n \quad \supset \quad c(\delta, m) = c(\sigma, m). \quad (BL5)$$

In the medium liveness specifications we defined the auxiliary function *Trying-ToReceive*, which indicated that the *reader* was waiting to receive a message. We now define the auxiliary function *WantToRead* that indicates when the *writer* is trying receive a message from the *buf* monitor. The *buf* monitor's first commitment describes when messages sent to *buf* are transferred to the *writer*:

$$c(\sigma, m) = k \wedge \Box\Diamond(WantToRead) \quad \supset \quad \Diamond\big(c(\psi, m) = k\big). \qquad (BL6)$$

The *buf* monitor provides two services: *send* and *receive*.

send(m)

live: $\Box\Diamond(\sim buf.full) \quad \supset \quad \Diamond(after\ buf.send) \wedge \Diamond(\sim buf.empty)$

receive(var m)

live: $\Diamond(buf.WantToRead) \quad \wedge$
$\big(\Diamond(\sim buf.empty) \quad \supset \quad \Diamond(after\ buf.receive) \wedge \Diamond(\sim buf.full)\big)$

We have assumed that only the *writer* can execute the *receive* operation and that only the *writer* can cause *WantToRead* to become true. These assumptions are stated as

$$\sim buf.empty \wedge \Box(\sim writer\ after\ receive) \quad \supset \quad \Box(\sim buf.empty)$$
$$\sim WantToRead \wedge \Box(\sim writer\ after\ receive) \quad \supset \quad \Box(\sim WantToRead).$$

The second commitment relates *WantToRead* to *full*:

$$\Box\Diamond(WantToRead) \quad \supset \quad \Box\Diamond(\sim buf.full). \qquad (BL7)$$

6.7.8. Liveness: Node Components

Inputs and Outputs

The liveness specification of the *inputs* and *outputs* monitors require two additional invariants. They specify the lengths of the histories β, γ, *inc*, and *outc* when the conditions for which the monitors wait are true:

$$hold[x] \neq empty \quad \supset \quad |\beta^x| = |inc[x]| + 1 \qquad (IL1)$$
$$ready[x] \quad \supset \quad |\gamma^x| = |outc[x]| + 1. \qquad (OL1)$$

The service specification for the *send* and *receive* operations follow immediately from the code of the corresponding procedures. The *receive* operation sends a request (incrementing the length of η^x from k to $k+1$); and if it ever receives a response (so that β^x has length $k+1$), then it will terminate. The *send* operation is similar. If a request ever arrives, then the response will be sent, and the *send* operation will terminate. The hypotheses require that $\square\lozenge(\sim buf.full)$ be true, otherwise the procedures could block at the *buf.send* operation.

Services of the *inputs* monitor:

receive(x; var v)

> live: $|inc[x]| = k \wedge \square\lozenge(\sim buf.full) \quad \supset$
> $\lozenge(|\eta^x| = k+1) \quad \wedge \quad (\lozenge(|\beta^x| = k+1) \supset \lozenge(after\ receive))$

response(m)

> live: $\lozenge(after\ response)$

Services of the *outputs* monitor:

send(x,v)

> live: $|outc[x]| = k \wedge \square\lozenge(\sim buf.full) \quad \supset$
> $(\lozenge(|\gamma^x| = k+1) \quad \supset \quad (\lozenge(after\ send) \wedge \lozenge(|\theta^x| = k+1)))$

6.7.9. Liveness: Node

request(m)

   live: $\Diamond$(*after request*)

6.7.9. Liveness: Node

The organization of the system liveness proof will be similar to that of the system safety proof. In this section we build node commitments out of submodule assertions; our goal is to relate the input histories of the node to the output histories of the node. As in Section 6.7.4, the input history can be α or $outc$, and the output history can be ω or inc.

If node n is the *sender* of channel x, then the live-assertion for *inputs.receive* states

$$at\ n.inputs.receive(x,v) \wedge |n.inc[x]| = k \wedge \Box\Diamond(\sim n.buf.full) \quad \supset \tag{1}$$
$$\Diamond(|n.\eta^x| = k+1).$$

Invariant I4 guarantees that all messages of $n.\eta^x$ are requests for channel x. We abbreviate such requests as $M_x^?$; we shall abbreviate responses on channel x as $M_x^!$. Assertion (1) implies that

$$at\ n.inputs.receive(x,v) \wedge |n.inc[x]| = k \wedge \Box\Diamond(\sim n.buf.full) \quad \supset$$
$$\Diamond\big(c(n.\eta, M_x^?) = k+1\big).$$

The history η merges into σ; using invariant BL3 (and our safety proof that neither δ nor θ contain $M_c^?$) we conclude

$$at\ n.inputs.receive(x,v) \wedge |n.inc[x]| = k \wedge \Box\Diamond(\sim n.buf.full) \quad \supset$$
$$\Diamond\big(c(n.\sigma, M_x^?) = k+1\big).$$

If we further assume that $\Box\Diamond(n.buf.WantToRead)$, then commitment BL6 implies that the requests are eventually read by the *writer*:

$$\big(n = receiver(x) \wedge at\ n.inputs.receive(x,v) \wedge |n.inc[x]| = k \wedge$$
$$\Box\Diamond(\sim n.buf.full) \wedge \Box\Diamond(n.buf.WantToRead)\big) \quad \supset$$
$$\Diamond\big(c(n.\psi, M_x^?) = k+1\big).$$

Commitment WL1 permits us to replace the assumption $\Box\Diamond buf.WantToRead$ with $\Box\Diamond bout.TryingToRead$; commitment WL2 then implies that node n will

6.7.9. Liveness: Node

eventually make the messages available to bout.

$$
\begin{aligned}
\big(n = receiver(z) \wedge at\ n.inputs.receive(z, v) \wedge |n.inc[z]| = k\ \wedge \\
\Box\Diamond(\sim n.buf.full) \wedge \Box\Diamond(n.bout.TryingToRead)\big) \supset \\
\Diamond\big(c(n.\omega, M_z^?) = k + 1\big),
\end{aligned}
\qquad (NL1)
$$

which is our first node commitment.

The derivation of the other node commitments are similar to that of NL1; they follow directly from the commitments and live-assertions of the node submodules. The remaining node commitments are:

$$
\begin{aligned}
\big(n \neq receiver(z) \wedge n \neq sender(z) \wedge c(n.\alpha, M_z^?) = k\ \wedge \\
\Box\Diamond(\sim n.buf.full) \wedge \Box\Diamond(n.bout.TryingToRead)\big) \supset \\
\Diamond\big(c(n.\omega, M_z^?) = k\big)
\end{aligned}
\qquad (NL2)
$$

$$
\begin{aligned}
\big(n = sender(z) \wedge at\ n.outputs.send(z, v) \wedge |n.outc[z]| = k\ \wedge \\
\Diamond\big(c(\alpha, M_z^?) = k + 1\big) \wedge \Box\Diamond(\sim n.buf.full)\big) \supset \\
\Diamond\big(after\ n.outputs.send(z, v)\big)
\end{aligned}
\qquad (NL3)
$$

$$
\begin{aligned}
\big(n = sender(z) \wedge at\ n.outputs.send(z, v) \wedge |n.outc[z]| = k\ \wedge \\
\Diamond\big(c(\alpha, M_z^?) = k + 1\big) \wedge \\
\Box\Diamond(\sim n.buf.full) \wedge \Box\Diamond(n.bout.TryingToRead)\big) \supset \\
\Diamond\big(c(\omega, M_z^!) = k + 1\big)
\end{aligned}
\qquad (NL4)
$$

$$
\begin{aligned}
\big(n \neq receiver(z) \wedge n \neq sender(z) \wedge c(n.\alpha, M_z^!) = k\ \wedge \\
\Box\Diamond(\sim n.buf.full) \wedge \Box\Diamond(n.bout.TryingToRead)\big) \supset \\
\Diamond\big(c(n.\omega, M_z^!) = k\big)
\end{aligned}
\qquad (NL5)
$$

$$
\begin{aligned}
\big(n = receiver(z) \wedge at\ n.inputs.receive(z, v) \wedge |n.inc[z]| = k\ \wedge \\
\Diamond\big(c(\alpha, M_z^!) = k + 1\big) \wedge \Box\Diamond(\sim n.buf.full)\big) \supset \\
\Diamond\big(after\ n.inputs.receive(z, v)\big).
\end{aligned}
\qquad (NL6)
$$

This completes the node commitments. In the next section we show that the assumptions $\Box\Diamond(\sim buf.full)$ and $\Box\Diamond(bout.TryingToRead)$ are valid, which will simplify the node liveness commitments. In Section 6.7.11, we will combine the node liveness assertions to prove the system commitment.

6.7.10. Liveness: No Blocking

6.7.10. Liveness: No Blocking

All of the node liveness commitments in the previous section included assumptions about the status of *buf*; three of the commitments included assumptions about the status of the *bout* medium.

Our goal in this section is to prove that for all nodes n

$$\Box\Diamond(\sim n.buf.full). \qquad (NL7)$$

Then we shall be able to deduce that for all nodes n

$$\Box\Diamond(\sim n.bin.TryingToReceive) \qquad (NL8)$$

as an immediate consequence of RL1 and NL7. Commitments NL7 and NL8 will simplify the six node liveness commitments.

▶**Proof of** NL7:

We first show that there is at most one outstanding message per channel. Invariants N14 and N15 state

$$n = receiver(x) \supset outstanding(n, x) \le 1$$

$$n \ne receiver(x) \supset outstanding(n, x) \le 0.$$

In other words, only the *receiver(x)* can send more messages to the network than it has received, and it can only send one more. That implies that there is at most one outstanding message per channel.

We next show that it is impossible for k nodes, where $k < nmax$, to have buffers that are perpetually full. Suppose that there are k such nodes; there exists a node, n, such that,

$$\Diamond\Box(n.buf.full) \wedge \sim \Diamond\Box((n \oplus 1).buf.full).$$

Commitment RL1 for node $n \oplus 1$ promises that the *reader* is infinitely often trying to receive a message from the medium:

$$\Box\Diamond((n \oplus 1).bin.TryingToReceive).$$

Assertion WL1 for the *writer* of node n then implies that

$$\Box\Diamond(n.buf.WantToRead).$$

6.7.11. Liveness: System

Finally, commitment BL7 of node n contradicts our assumption by promising that

$$\Box\Diamond(\sim n.buf.full).$$

Therefore, it is impossible for some, but not all, of the nodes in the network to be permanently blocked.

The last step in proving NL7 is to show that it is impossible for all the nodes in the system to be permanently blocked. Suppose that $\forall n(\Diamond\Box n.buf.full)$. We know that if the $buf.full$ then there are $bmax$ messages in buf (BL2). If all of the buffers are full, then there are $nmax \times bmax$ outstanding messages. The definition of $bmax$ implies that $nmax \times bmax > cmax$. We have already proved, however, that there can be at most one outstanding message per channel—a maximum of $cmax$ messages outstanding for the entire system. Hence, not all of the buffers can be full at the same time. ∎

6.7.11. Liveness: System

We wish to prove that if the sending user and the receiving user of channel x start to send and receive a message, then they both will terminate. In other words, the calls to *inputs.receive* and *outputs.send* implement, at a higher level, the calls to the node's *send* and *receive* operations. The safety properties of these high-level operations are the same as the safety properties of their implementations: after termination the associated history has increased by the message sent or received. In effect, we are trying to show that the live-assertion for these high-level operations imply that the operations terminate unconditionally:

$$a \text{ at } receiver(x).receive(x, v) \wedge b \text{ at } sender(x).send(x, v) \quad \supset$$
$$\Diamond(x \text{ after receive}) \wedge \Diamond(y \text{ after send}),$$

where a is the receiving user and b is the sending user. Rather than work out the detail of specifying these high-level operations, we prove the same property of the implementing operations:

$$a \text{ at } receiver(x).inputs.receive(x) \wedge b \text{ at } sender(x).outputs.send(x) \quad \supset$$
$$\Diamond(x \text{ after receive}) \wedge \Diamond(y \text{ after send}).$$

$$(SL1)$$

The proof of SL1 follows quickly from the node assertions.

We first show that when the receiving user is *at receive*, the input and output histories of the channel are equal in length:

$$\text{at } receiver(x).receive(x, v) \supset receiver(x).inc[x] = sender(x).outc[x]. \quad (S3)$$

6.7.11. Liveness: System

▶**Proof of S3:**

We prove S3 only for the case that $receiver(x) \neq sender(x)$. The other case is similar. Invariant N12 states that

$$at\ receiver(x).receive(x, c)\ \supset\ |receiver(x).inc[x]| \geq |receiver(x).\omega^x|.$$

For the nodes between the *receiver* and the *sender*, invariants N1 and M1 imply

$$|receiver(x).\omega^x| \geq |sender(x).\alpha^x|.$$

N6 then implies
$$|sender(x).\alpha^x| \geq |sender(x).outc[x]|.$$

But S1 implies

$$|sender(x).outc[x]| \geq |receiver(x).inc[x]|,$$

which implies that $inc[x] = outc[x]$. ∎

▶**Proof of SL1:**

We assume that a is at *inputs.receive* and that b is at *outputs.send* on the appropriate nodes. Let k be the initial length of the *inc* and *outc* histories, which are the same by S3. Commitment NL1 implies that eventually the request is sent by $receiver(x)$:

$$\Diamond(c(receiver(x).\omega, M_x^!) = k + 1).$$

Commitment ML3 then implies that the request is sent to the next node:

$$\Diamond(c((receiver(x) \oplus 1).\alpha, M_x^!) = k + 1).$$

For each node n between $receiver(x)$ and $sender(x)$, commitments NL2 and ML3 imply that the request is passed along:

$$\Diamond(c((n \oplus 1).\alpha, M_x^!) = k + 1).$$

At the $sender(x)$ node, commitment NL3 implies that the *send* operation terminates:

$$\Diamond(after\ sender(x).outputs.send(x, v)).$$

6.7.11. Liveness: System

Commitment NL4 also implies that the response is eventually sent:

$$\Diamond\big(c(sender(z).\omega, M'_z) = k+1\big).$$

Commitment ML3 then implies that the response is forwarded to the next node:

$$\Diamond\big(c((sender(z) \oplus 1).\alpha, M'_z) = k+1\big).$$

For each node n between $sender(z)$ and $receiver(z)$ commitments NL5 and ML3 imply

$$\Diamond\big(c((n \oplus 1).\alpha, M'_z) = k+1\big).$$

Finally, back at $receiver(z)$, commitment NL6 implies that the *receive* operation terminates:

$$\Diamond\big(after\ receiver(z).inputs.receive(z,v)\big). \qquad \blacksquare$$

The proof of Brinch Hansen's network does not differ from the proofs of Stenning's protocol and the alternating bit protocol in the techniques that are used, but rather in the amount of detail that is required. At each level of the system, we produce assertions that can require assumptions about the operation of the next higher level. As the number of levels grow, the complexity increases. What makes the multi-level proof practical, is that at each level we can compensate for the detail of the extra assumptions by hiding much of the detail of the underlying implementation.

Chapter 7
Resource Allocation

In Chapter 6, we verified properties of network protocols. The structure of these protocols was simple, a number of independent processors tied together by relatively simple communication media. Other kinds of parallel programs are not as easily decomposed into independent modules. For example, one of the main services of an operating system is the allocation of system resources to users; this task is called *resource allocation*. Programs that implement and use resource allocation entail a greater sharing of modules than do protocols; this sharing results in a greater vulnerability to interference and deadlock. Proving even simple properties of resource allocators can be difficult because of this complexity. In Section 7.1, we motivate the need for resource allocation. In Section 7.2, we present Hoare's structured paging system, which is a complex example, with many levels of abstraction. By specifying and verifying Hoare's system, we show that the techniques developed in this thesis apply to the verification of complex systems.

7.1. Introduction

Consider a system with five tape drives. Users of this system control one, two, or three tape drives at a time, but each tape drive can have only one user at any moment. To prevent interference in the use of a drive, some mutual-exclusion protection is needed. We present three possible schemes. In the first solution, all of the drives are protected by a single monitor. The built-in mutual-exclusion properties of the monitor prevent any interference. However, such a solution does not permit the maximum use of the tape drives; multiple users cannot access different drives simultaneously because only one process can own the monitor at a time. Our second solution is to provide one monitor for each drive. In this case, two users still cannot access a single drive simultaneously. The fault of our first solution is also corrected: more than one user can access the set of drives simultaneously. This solution, however, has a different drawback. To obtain control of more than one drive, a user gains control of one drive at a time; this strategy leads to the possibility of deadlock. In the first two solutions, mutual exclusion is enforced syntactically with monitors: no access is allowed to a tape drive except by using a monitor procedure and only one procedure of a given monitor can be executed at any one time. The third solution involves a resource allocation module to guarantee mutual exclusion. Users submit sets of requests to the allocator. Whenever an entire set of requests for a user can be satisfied, the allocator grants that user the right to use the desired subset of the tape drives. The user can then access the allocated drives without referencing the allocator, leaving the allocator free to handle other *request* and *release* operations. When the user is finished, it releases control of the tape drives by another call to the resource allocator. We assume that users only access the tape drives when they have permission to do so from the allocator. If we can prove that the allocator never assigns one resource to two users, then we have guaranteed mutual exclusion. Even though the allocator is a single monitor protecting all of the tape drives, it does not have the same defect as does the first solution because the allocator only handles requests and releases; it does not mediate the use of the tape drives themselves. The allocator avoids the drawback of the second solution by never allocating partial requests and thereby avoiding deadlocks.

The tape drive example is extremely simple. More interesting examples of this class of problem include managing disk space, providing shared buffers in main memory, and managing large databases with multiple access paths. Even more intriguing are problems in distributed management, where different resources are allocated by programs on different processors. For a further discussion of various resource allocation programs, see Owicki [36]. In the next section, we present Hoare's algorithm to manage a main memory and a drum so as to provide a large virtual memory.

7.2. Hoare's Structured Paging System

In 1973, Hoare [17] demonstrated that structured programming techniques were applicable to a parallel environment by describing a structured paging system. The system allows for the sharing of a main memory and a backing store among several users. The backing store resembles a sectored drum or any device with a fixed page size. Hoare's system is complex and is intended to be efficient in the use of both memories. Section 7.2.1 describes the system and presents an outline of the rest of this chapter.

This section is organized differently than those of the previous chapter. In Chapter 6, we first presented the code for the components of a protocol. The media that had no code were also described. We then derived invariants, commitments, and service assertions for each component of the system. Finally, we combined these component properties to form system properties. For Hoare's system, in contrast, we shall include no code. A VALET implementation can be found in Appendix B, but this section will concentrate on the formal specification and the proof of the system using invariants, commitments, and service

7.2.1. Overview

assertions. All of the assertions can be derived from the code in the appendix, but the reader should be able to understand the system from the diagrams, which show the components and their interconnections, and from the formal specifications. The presentation will begin by specifying high-level modules. Next, the components of these modules will be specified. We shall then prove that the submodules correctly implement the high-level modules. Section 7.2.1 describes Hoare's system and the organization of the rest of this chapter.

7.2.1. Overview

In order to prove the correctness of Hoare's system, we must state the problem that the system is intended to solve. Such a specification has two parts: the desired high-level services that are to be provided to the users and the primitive operations with which we can implement these services. In this section, we present an overview of the problem and the organization of the solution. At the end of this section we enumerate the differences between our solution and that of Hoare.

The system is built upon two primitive data structures: a main memory and a drum. The main memory is called *MainStore*; it is an array consisting of M pages. Each page is an array with C words (cells). The drum memory is called *DrumStore*; it also contains D pages with C words per page. Our goal is to provide a virtual memory of V pages for a number of users. The address space of the virtual memory is much larger than the that of the main memory, but less than that of the drum:

$$D > V \gg M$$

type

    MainPageFrame = 0 .. M-1
    DrumPageFrame = 0 .. D-1
    VirtualPageFrame = 0 .. V-1
    cell = 0 .. C-1
    word = { one machine word }
    page = array cell of word

var

    MainStore: **array** *MainPageFrame* **of** *page*
    DrumStore: **array** *DrumPageFrame* **of** *page*

7.2.1. Overview

Our virtual memory must allow different virtual pages to be accessed simultaneously, but access to a single page is restricted to one operation at a time. Furthermore, the virtual pages must be distinct; changing an element of virtual page i cannot affect the contents of virtual page j, where $j \neq i$. We are to provide three operations to the users of the virtual memory: *fetch*, *assign*, and *clear*. The operation $fetch(v, l, w)$ will result in variable w receiving the value of of word l of virtual page v. Similarly, $assign(v, l, w)$ causes word l of virtual page v to take on the value w. The $clear(v)$ operation will be used to set all the elements of page v to zero.

The *MainStore* is an array of *shared* pages. The individual pages of *MainStore* can be used by more than one process, but they are not protected by a monitor. Up to this point in the thesis, all data objects that were not local to one process were required to be protected by a monitor. Relaxing this rule complicates the proof process, but it does not present insurmountable problems. We are provided with five primitive operations that can access *MainStore*: fetch a word, store a word, clear a page, copy a page from the drum, and copy a page to the drum. All five operations are considered to be atomic: they cannot interfere with each other, and they cannot be interrupted. They are all guaranteed to terminate. The first three operations (*fetch*, *assign*, and *clear*) are called by the module that implements the virtual memory. The last two operations (*CopyMtoD* and *CopyDtoM*) can only be called by the module that implements the drum. The specification of the *MainStore* operations is presented is Section 7.2.3.

The *DrumStore* is also an array of pages, but no access is allowed to individual words of a drum page. The actions of the drum and the synchronizing of drum requests will be handled by a *drum* module. The *drum* module provides two operations: *input* and *output*. A call to the *input* operation represents a request to the *drum* module to copy a page from the *DrumStore* to the *MainStore*; a call to *output* is request to copy a *MainStore* to the *DrumStore*. Further details on this module are discussed in Section 7.2.4.

Hoare's system comprises five modules: *VirtualMemory*, *MFree*, *DFree*, *drum*, and *MainStore*. The users will call the *VirtualMemory* module with the *fetch*, *assign*, and *clear* operations. The specification of the *VirtualMemory* module can be found in Section 7.2.5; its implementation can be found in Section 7.2.6. Figure 7.2–1 is a diagram of Hoare's system.

The *VirtualMemory* module can access the *MainStore* and the *drum* module. To control access to the two stores, there are two resource allocators: *MFree* and *DFree*. The *MFree* monitor allocates *MainStore* pages, and the *DFree* monitor allocates the *DrumStore* pages. The resource allocators are discussed in Section 7.2.2.

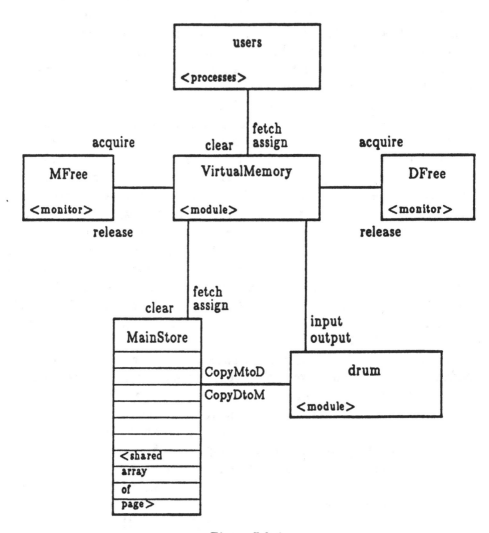

Figure 7.2-1
Hoare's Structured Paging System

7.2.1. Overview

The *VirtualMemory* module comprises the *VirtualStore* and the *Cyclic-Discarder*. The *VirtualStore* is an array of *VirtualPage* modules. The *Virtual-Page* modules are specified as part of the implementation of the *VirtualMemory* module in Section 7.2.6. The implementation of the *VirtualPage* module is presented in Section 7.2.7. The *CyclicDiscarder* repeatedly signals each virtual page, requesting that the contents of its *MainStore* page (if any) be move to the *DrumStore* and the *MainStore* page be released. This action prevents deadlock over the use of the *MainStore*.

The remainder of Section 7.2.1 describes the difference between the specification presented in this thesis and Hoare's original algorithm.

Differences Between Hoare's Solution and Ours

Our solution to the virtual page system differs from Hoare's in three ways: we have left out some of the operations of Hoare's solution, we have changed the implementation slightly to accommodate VALET, and we have changed one significant aspect of the implementation.

Hoare's system contains three services that are not included in our solution. Two of the features were attempts at increased efficiency of the system. They were variable load control to prevent thrashing and a use-bit to implement a modified least-recently-used *CyclicDiscarder*. The third feature was the ability to lock a main memory page in place, so that the *CyclicDiscarder* could not transfer that page to the drum and release the *MainStore* page. This final feature made the prevention of deadlock a user responsibility rather than a *VirtualMemory* responsibility, and we preferred to include deadlock prevention in the implementation.

As regards VALET, Hoare's solution is modified to replace *wait* and *signal* operations with wait statements using boolean expressions. Hoare also includes the initialization of a process as part of one of his procedures; we achieve the same effect with a process and monitor pair (*boss* and *clerk*).

The major change that we have made to Hoare's system is to cause the *CyclicDiscarder* to cycle though the virtual pages in its attempt to send idle pages to the drum, rather than to cycle through the *MainStore* pages. Hoare's solution is obviously more efficient; why bother to signal every virtual page, when only a small fraction of them control resident *MainStore* pages? Hoare's solution, however, requires operations to initiate and cancel the execution of one process by another process (in order to coordinate the clearing of a page and the automatic discarding of a page). Without such an ability as an atomic operation, the system becomes more complicated and much more difficult to prove. Our interest in this problem is resource allocation, not dynamic process structures. The modification does not affect the resource allocation aspects of the system.

7.2.2. Resource Allocators: MFree and DFree

Each allocator consists of a pool of the indices of the unused pages. The pool represents the physical (main or drum) pages that are not currently assigned to a virtual page. Each allocator maintains an auxiliary set *owns* for each virtual page. The *owns* set contains the indices of the physical pages that belong to each virtual page. We shall abbreviate *MFree.owns*[v], which is the private set of virtual page v, as *Mowns*[v]. Similarly *DFree.owns*[v] is abbreviated as *Downs*[v]. Below, we specify only the *MFree* monitor; the specification of the *DFree* monitor is similar.

The *MFree* monitor provides three visible operations: *empty*, *acquire*, and *release*. The auxiliary function *empty* is true if there are no free pages left in the pool (m ranges over *MainPageFrame* and v, v' range over *VirtualPageFrame*):

$$MFree.empty \equiv (\forall m\,(\exists v\,(m \in Mowns[v]))). \qquad (MF1)$$

The second invariant states that each physical page can be assigned to at most one virtual page.:

$$\forall m\,(\exists v\,(m \in Mowns[v]) \quad \supset \quad \exists! v\,(m \in Mowns[v])). \qquad (MF2)$$

The services that the monitor provides are *acquire* and *release*. The *acquire* operation can block if there are no free pages. The release operation always terminates. (The "$-$" operator represents set difference.)

MFree.acquire(var m)

```
pre:    Mowns[id] = X
post:   m ∈ Mowns[id]   ∧   Mowns[id] − m = X
live:   □◇(∼ MFree.empty)   ⊃   ◇(after MFree.acquire)
```

7.2.2. Resource Allocators: MFree and DFree

MFree.release(m)

pre: $\quad m \in Mowns[\text{id}] \quad \wedge \quad Mowns[\text{id}] - m = X$

post: $\quad Mowns[\text{id}] = X$

live: $\quad \Diamond(\text{after } MFree.release) \wedge \Diamond(\sim MFree.empty)$

We restrict the operation of the monitor so that only *acquire* and *release* can affect *empty*:

$$MFree.empty \wedge \Box(\sim \text{after } MFree.release) \quad \supset \quad \Box(MFree.empty)$$

$$\sim MFree.empty \wedge \Box(\sim \text{after } MFree.acquire) \quad \supset \quad \Box(\sim MFree.empty).$$

Page Ownership and Locality

In the upcoming sections we shall discuss copying pages from *DrumStore* to *MainStore*, copying pages from *MainStore* to *DrumStore*, and modifying pages of *MainStore*. When specifying these operations, we would like to refer to the values of the *MainStore* and the *DrumStore* before and after the operation. Under the current rules for stating pre- and post-assertions, we are not allowed to refer to any variables that are not local or private to the calling process, as the value of non-private variables can be changed by other processes. On the other hand, we know that as long as a virtual page has permission to use a page of *MainStore* (or of *DrumStore*), no other virtual page will have permission to use that same page (MF2 and DF2). We shall require, therefore, every procedure that virtual page v calls to modify $MainStore[m]$ have the assertion $m \in Mowns[v]$ as a precondition. Similarly, every procedure that modifies $DrumStore[d]$ must have the assertion $d \in Downs[v]$ as a precondition. As long as the *MainStore* page and the *DrumStore* page are controlled by a particular virtual page, invariants MF2 and DF2 will permit us to consider the physical pages as being "private" to the calling virtual page. In essence, we are using an invariant to justify locality assumptions that have previously been guaranteed syntactically.

7.2.3. Main Store

The *MainStore* is an array of *shared* pages. There are five (atomic) primitive operations with which to access *MainStore*: fetch a word, store a word, clear a page, copy a page from the drum, and copy a page to the drum. The first three operations are called by the *VirtualMemory* module. The last two operations can only be called by the *drum* module.

The *MainStore* serves the *VirtualMemory* module with three operations: *fetch*, *assign*, and *clear*. All three operations are guaranteed to terminate. The operation *fetch*(m, l, w) returns in variable w the value of *MainStore*$[m, l]$. Similarly, the operation *assign*(m, l, w) stores the value of expression w into *MainStore*$[m, l]$. The *clear*(m) operation sets the value of all words in page m of *MainStore* to zero. In the service specification below, the notation X_i^j represents the value of array X with the value of element $X[i]$ replace by the expression j.

MainStore.fetch(m, l, w)

    pre: $m \in Mowns[id] \wedge MainStore[m] = M$
    post: $MainStore[m] = M \wedge w = MainStore[m, l]$
    live: $\Diamond(after\ MainStore.fetch)$

MainStore.assign(m, l, w)

    pre: $m \in Mowns[id] \wedge MainStore[m] = M$
    post: $MainStore[m] = M_l^w$
    live: $\Diamond(after\ MainStore.assign)$

MainStore.clear(m)

    pre: $m \in Mowns[id]$
    post: $\forall i\ (MainStore[m, i] = 0)$
    live: $\Diamond(after\ MainStore.clear)$

The auxiliary constant id represents the index of the calling virtual page.

As we mentioned above, these pre- and post-assertions are not completely rigorous, because $m \in Mowns[id]$ does not imply that *MainStore*$[m]$ is truly local to the calling process. If we are not careful, this relaxation of our rules could cause problems with the proof of the calling process. In general, a post condition of a monitor call can be used in the proof of the calling process as long as the variables of the post-condition are not changed by the calling process. With our relaxed rules, we must not make use of the value of *MainStore*$[m]$ after m has been released to *Mowns*, even though there has been no explicit change to the *MainStore* page.

7.2.4. Drum Module

The *MainStore* provides the *drum* module with two services: *CopyDtoM* and *CopyMtoD*. The specification of the primitive drum/memory transfer operations are as follows.

MainStore.CopyDtoM(d, m)

    pre: $m \in Mowns[id] \land d \in Downs[id] \land DrumStore[d] = D$
    post: $MainStore[m] = D = DrumStore[d]$
    live: $\Diamond(after\ MainStore.CopyDtoM)$

MainStore.CopyMtoD(m, d)

    pre: $m \in Mowns[id] \land d \in Downs[id] \land MainStore[m] = M$
    post: $DrumStore[d] = M = MainStore[m]$
    live: $\Diamond(after\ MainStore.CopyMtoD)$

All five services are defined to be atomic. It is rather disquieting, however, to require such large operations as copying a page to be atomic. Now that we have specified the resource allocators and have required the appropriate preconditions on the transfer and clear operations, we need not consider the page-level operations to be atomic in their own right; they are atomic in effect, because no other process can access a page for which it does not have permission.

7.2.4. Drum Module

The drum is a shared resource with one channel to the *MainStore*; therefore, only one page can be transferred to or from the drum at a time. The *drum* module provides two services to the *VirtualMemory* module: *input* and *output*. A virtual page executes the operation *input(m, d)* to copy page *d* of the *DrumStore* to page *m* of the *MainStore*. Similarly the operation *output(d, m)* will copy *MainStore[m]* to *DrumStore[d]*. The *drum* module consists of one process and one monitor. The *drummer* monitor implements the *input* and *output* services of the module. It also schedules the requests for the drum transfers. The *DrumHardware* process is the active component of the module; it services the requests that are scheduled by the *drummer*. The *drum* module is shown in Figure 7.2-2. Below we discuss the specification of the module's services and the implementation of these services by the *drummer* and the *DrumHardware*. Finally, we prove that the *drummer* and the *DrumHardware* correctly implement the *drum* module services.

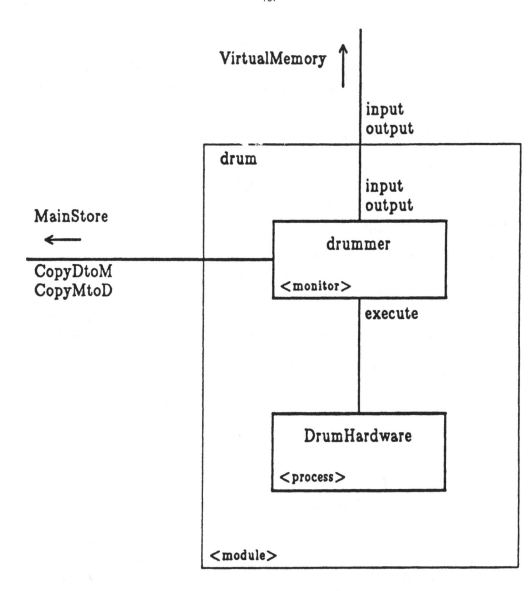

Figure 7.2–2
The Drum Module

7.2.4. Drum Module

Drum Module Specification

Our goal is to have the *drum* module provide two services to the *Virtual-Memory* module, *input* and *output*. Because these operations will affect pages of both *MainStore* and *DrumStore*, we require that the calling virtual page have permission to access both physical pages to be used. At the end of this section we show that the implementation of these services matches the specifications below.

drum.input(m, d)

    pre: $m \in Mowns[id] \land d \in Downs[id] \land DrumStore[d] = D$
    post: $MainStore[m] = D = DrumStore[d]$
    live: $\Diamond$(after drum.input)

drum.output(d, m)

    pre: $d \in Downs[id] \land m \in Mowns[id] \land MainStore[m] = M$
    post: $DrumStore[d] = M = MainStore[m]$
    live: $\Diamond$(after drum.output)

Drum Implementation: The Drummer Monitor

The *drummer* monitor provides three services: *input*, *output*, and *execute*. The first two procedures directly implement the module services with the same names:

$$drum.input(m, d) \quad \equiv \quad drummer.input(m, d)$$

$$drum.output(m, d) \quad \equiv \quad drummer.output(m, d).$$

The *execute* service can be called only by the *DrumHardware*. The monitor contains one visible auxiliary function: *finished*.

The command *input*(m, d) waits until the drum is not in use; it then records the request that page d of the *DrumStore* is to be copied into page m of the *MainStore*. After recording the request it waits until the *DrumHardware* sets *finished* equal to true, indicating that the transfer is complete. Then, the *input* command indicates that the drum is not in use, and release the *drummer* monitor. The *output* command is similar, except that its request is that page m of the *MainStore* be copied into page d of the *DrumStore*.

The *execute* command can be called only by the *DrumHardware*. The action of *execute* depends upon the outstanding request: an outstanding input causes the appropriate *DrumStore* page to be transferred to *MainStore*, an

7.2.4. Drum Module

outstanding output causes the appropriate *MainStore* page to be transferred to the *DrumStore*, and if there are no outstanding requests then nothing is transferred. In all cases, *execute* causes *finished* to be true. The specification of the drummer services is as follows.

drummer.input(m,d)

pre:	$m \in Mowns[id] \wedge d \in Downs[id] \wedge DrumStore[s] = D$
post:	$MainStore[m] = D = DrumStore[d]$
live:	$\Box\Diamond(drummer.finished) \quad \supset \quad \Diamond(after\ drummer.input)$

drummer.output(d,m)

pre:	$d \in Downs[id] \wedge m \in Mowns[id] \wedge MainStore[s] = M$
post:	$DrumStore[d] = M = MainStore[m]$
live:	$\Box\Diamond(drummer.finished) \quad \supset \quad \Diamond(after\ drummer.output)$

drummer.execute

pre:	*true*
post:	*true*
live:	$\Diamond(after\ drummer.execute) \wedge \Diamond(drummer.finished)$

We also restrict the the auxiliary function *finished*, so that only *input* and *output* can cause it to become false:

$$finished \wedge \Box(\sim after\ input \wedge \sim after\ output) \quad \supset \quad \Box(finished).$$

Proving that these services are implemented by the code in the appendix requires another level of proof involving invariants of the internal variables of the monitor and the code of the monitor.

Drum Implementation: The DrumHardware Process

The *DrumHardware* process is an infinite loop, which repeatedly calls *execute*. The *execute* operation always terminates, and causes *finished* to become true, hence the drum hardware commitment is

$$\Box\Diamond(drummer.finished). \tag{DH1}$$

7.2.5. *Virtual Memory Specifications*

Drum: Specification Matches Implementation

Combining the *drummer* service specifications and the *DrumHardware* commitment, we can immediately deduce that the *drum* service specifications are implemented correctly.

7.2.5. Virtual Memory Specifications

The *VirtualMemory* module provides three services to the users: *fetch* (a word from a virtual page), *assign* (a value to a word of a virtual page) and *clear* (a virtual page). In this section, we specify the properties of these operations. In the next section, we discuss their implementation.

The liveness property of the module is expressed by the guarantee that all three operations terminate:

VirtualMemory.fetch(p,l,w)

   live: $\Diamond$(*after fetch*)

VirtualMemory.assign(p,l,w)

   live: $\Diamond$(*after assign*)

VirtualMemory.clear(p)

   live: $\Diamond$(*after clear*)

The system safety property is that the virtual memory mimics the properties of a *MainStore* of the same size. How do we state and prove this safety property?

To state the safety properties of a page of memory, we must know how the page is to be used. Because pages are not local to any one process, we can not, in general, use pre- and post- assertions to describe their safety properties. Only in the case that exactly one user has access to page (and hence the page is in some sense private to that user) can we state the safety properties as follows.

VirtualMemory.fetch(p,l,w)

   pre: $memory[p] = M$
   post: $memory[p] = M \wedge w = memory[p, l]$

VirtualMemory.assign(p,l,w)

   pre: $memory[p] = M$
   post: $memory[p] = M_l^w$

7.2.5. Virtual Memory Specifications

VirtualMemory.clear(p)

pre: *true*
post: $\forall i(memory[p, i] = 0)$

If the page is shared, then the pre- and post-assertions above are not valid, because the page is not local or private to the calling process. If we could prove that between an *assign* to a word and the subsequent *fetch* of the word by one process, no other process had modified that word, then we could use assertions similar to those given above. Another approach to specifying the safety of a page would be to record every change to that page in a history and state that *fetch* returns some value of the word that existed between the time that *fetch* was called and the time that the *fetch* operation terminated (stated in terms of the history of changes).

Rather than present a series of assumptions and the resulting safety properties, we leave the exact properties unspecified and state the following general property: any safety property that can be proved about a *MainStore* with V pages, can be prove about the *VirtualStore*. In other words, the *VirtualStore* is invisible to the calling process. Even though the representation of the *VirtualStore* page can migrate to and from the disk, from the users point of view its safety properties are identical to an array of V pages.

We state our safety property as follows. Assume that we have a program S that operates on the *VirtualMemory*, and that we want to prove that

$$\{P\}S\{Q\}.$$

We transform S into an equivalent program S'. The transformation replaces every access by S to *VirtualMemory* by a corresponding access to a shared *MainStore* with V pages. We then prove

$$\{P\}S'\{Q\}.$$

Our claim is that the safety property of the *VirtualMemory* system allows us to then conclude

$$\{P\}S\{Q\}.$$

We prove this claim at the end of Section 7.2.7.

7.2.6. Virtual Memory Implementation

7.2.6. Virtual Memory Implementation

The *VirtualMemory* module is composed of two submodules: the *Cyclic-Discarder* and the *VirtualStore*. The *VirtualStore* is an array of *VirtualPage* modules. The services of the *VirtualMemory* module are implemented by the operations of the *VirtualPage* modules:

$$VirtualMemory.fetch(v, l, w) \equiv VirtualStore[v].fetch(l, w)$$
$$VirtualMemory.assign(v, l, w) \equiv VirtualStore[v].assign(l, w)$$
$$VirtualMemory.clear(v) \equiv VirtualStore[v].clear.$$

The *CyclicDiscarder* is used to prevent deadlocks over the use of the *Main-Store*. The *CyclicDiscarder* signals each *VirtualPage* at regular intervals to indicate that the contents of the *MainStore* page that it controls, if any, should be stored on the drum and the *MainStore* page should be released. Figure 7.2–3 diagrams the *VirtualMemory* module.

In the remainder of this section, we will discuss the specification of the components of the *VirtualMemory* module. We first specify the properties of the *VirtualPage* modules that constitute the *VirtualStore*. We then specify the properties of the *CyclicDiscarder*. Finally, we show that these specifications imply the correctness of the *VirtualMemory* services.

Virtual Page Specifications

The elements of *VirtualStore* are *VirtualPage* modules, each of which provides three services to the users, one service to the *CyclicDiscarder*, and one auxiliary function. The user services were mentioned above: *fetch*, *assign*, and *clear*. For the *CyclicDiscarder* process, the *VirtualPage* module provides a *signal* operation, so that the *VirtualPage* can be informed when it should release its *MainStore* page. The specification of the services for the *VirtualPage* module *VirtualStore[s]* is listed below. (The discussion of safety properties has been postponed to the end of the next section).

VirtualStore[s].fetch(l,w)

   live: $\forall v \left(\Box \Diamond (VirtualStore[v].signalled) \right) \supset \Diamond (after\ VirtualStore[s].fetch)$

VirtualStore[s].assign(l,w)

   live: $\forall v \left(\Box \Diamond (VirtualStore[v].signalled) \right) \supset \Diamond (after\ VirtualStore[s].assign)$

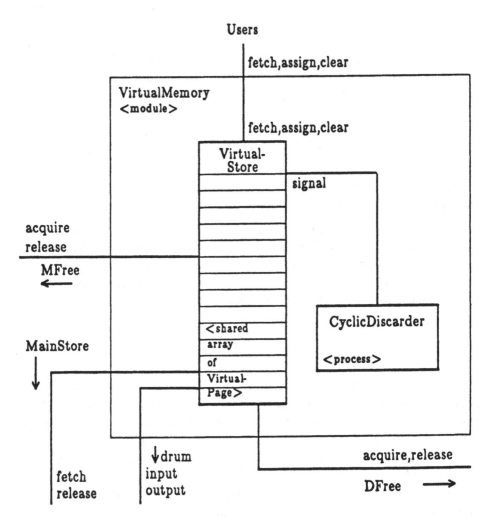

Figure 7.2–3
The Virtual Memory Module

7.2.6. Virtual Memory Implementation

VirtualStore[s].clear

  live: $\forall v \, (\Box\Diamond(VirtualStore[v].signalled)) \supset \Diamond(after\ VirtualStore[s].clear)$

VirtualStore[s].signal

  live: $\Diamond(after\ VirtualStore[s].signal) \wedge \Diamond(VirtualStore[s].signalled)$

We must also restrict changes in the value of the auxiliary function *signalled*:

$$VirtualStore[s].signalled \quad \wedge$$
$$\Box(\sim after\ VirtualStore[s].fetch \wedge \sim after\ VirtualStore[s].assign) \quad \supset$$
$$\Box(VirtualStore[s].signalled)$$

$$\sim VirtualStore[s].signalled \quad \wedge \quad \Box(\sim after\ VirtualStore[s].signal \quad \supset$$
$$\Box(\sim VirtualStore[s].signalled).$$

Note that the above specifications indicate that it is always permissible for the *CyclicDiscarder* to *signal* the *VirtualPage*, and that *signal* operation is guaranteed to terminate. In Section 7.2.8, we present the implementation of these operations and show that the implementation matches these specifications.

Cyclic Discarder Specifications

The *CyclicDiscarder* is a simple process that repeatedly calls *signal* on each *VirtualPage* module in *VirtualStore*. From the live-assertion of signal we can conclude the commitment

$$\forall v(\Box\Diamond(VirtualStore[v].signalled)).$$

Virtual Memory: Specification Matches Implementation

Having described the implementation of the *VirtualMemory* operations, we can prove that the implementation implies the specification of those operations. The live-assertions of the *VirtualMemory* services were as follows.

VirtualMemory.fetch(p,l,w)

  live: $\Diamond(after\ fetch)$

7.2.7. *Virtual Page Implementation*

VirtualMemory.assign(p,l,w)

   live: $\Diamond$(*after assign*)

VirtualMemory.clear(p)

   live: $\Diamond$(*after clear*)

    The validity of each specification is implied immediately by the specification of the corresponding *VirtualPage* module (*VirtualStore*[p]) and the specification of the *CyclicDiscarder*.

7.2.7. Virtual Page Implementation

    In this section, we specify the process and monitors that implement a *VirtualPage*. We then show that the specified components correctly implement the *VirtualPage* services, which were presented in Section 7.2.6. Finally, we discuss the safety properties of the *VirtualPage*.

    Each *VirtualPage* module consists of three submodules: two monitors and a process. The *VPage* monitor is the heart of the *VirtualPage* module; it implements the *VirtualPage* services *fetch*, *assign*, and *clear*:

$$
\begin{aligned}
VirtualPage.fetch(l, w) &\equiv VPage.fetch(l, w) \\
VirtualPage.assign(l, w) &\equiv VPage.assign(l, w) \\
VirtualPage.clear &\equiv VPage.clear.
\end{aligned}
$$

The *clerk* monitor receives the signals from the *CyclicDiscarder* that indicate that this *VirtualPage* should send its *MainStore* page back to the *DrumStore*. The *clerk* also provides the auxiliary function *signalled*:

$$
\begin{aligned}
VirtualPage.signal &\equiv clerk.signal \\
VirtualPage.signalled &\equiv clerk.signalled
\end{aligned}
$$

The *boss* process determines when to cause a *MainStore* page to be released on the basis of the signals received by the *clerk*. Figure 7.2–4 shows the structure of the *VirtualPage* module.

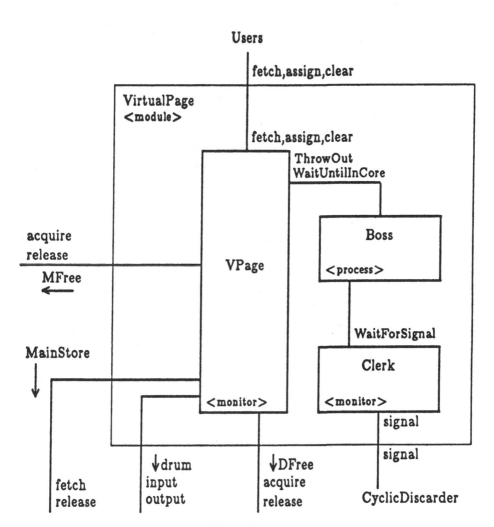

Figure 7.2–4
The Virtual Page Module

7.2.7. Virtual Page Implementation

VPage Specification

Three of the *VPage* services implement the corresponding *VirtualPage* services: *fetch*, *assign*, and *clear*. The *VPage* monitor also provides two services to the *boss* process, *WaitUntilInCore* and *ThrowOut*, and one auxiliary function, *InCore*.

A user indicates that it wants to perform an operation on a page of the *VirtualMemory* by calling one of the three *VirtualMemory* services. Each of these services is implemented by a corresponding *VirtualPage* service, which is implemented by a corresponding *VPage* service. If the service is a *fetch* or an *assign* then the *VPage* monitor checks to see if the contents of the virtual page are currently represented in the *MainStore*. If they are, then the operation is performed. Otherwise, either the page must be clear, or its contents must be on the drum. In either case, a request is issued to *MFree* for a free *MainStore* page. If the virtual page is clear, then the new *MainStore* page is cleared. If the virtual page was stored on the drum, then the contents of the drum page are copied into the new *MainStore* page. The user's operation is then performed.

The liveness specification of the *VPage* include the five service specifications, two invariants, and one commitment (along with some restrictions on the auxiliary functions). Each of the service specifications contains a hypothesis concerning the values of *DFree.empty*, *MFree.empty*, and *InCore*. These hypotheses are sufficient to prove that none of the five operations can be blocked on internal monitor calls. (This is necessary because if one operation became blocked on a call to *MFree.acquire*, for example, then no other operation could gain access to the *VPage* monitor.) The discussion of the safety properties can be found at the end of this section.

VPage.fetch(c,w)

live: $\Box\Diamond(\sim DFree.empty) \land \left(\Box\Diamond(\sim MFree.empty) \lor \Diamond\Box(InCore)\right) \quad \supset$
$\Diamond(after\ fetch) \land \Diamond(InCore)$

VPage.assign(c,w)

live: $\Box\Diamond(\sim DFree.empty) \land \left(\Box\Diamond(\sim MFree.empty) \lor \Diamond\Box(InCore)\right) \quad \supset$
$\Diamond(after\ assign) \land \Diamond(InCore)$

VPage.clear

live: $\Box\Diamond(\sim DFree.empty) \land \left(\Box\Diamond(\sim MFree.empty) \lor \Diamond\Box(InCore)\right) \quad \supset$
$\Diamond(after\ clear) \land \Diamond(cleared)$

7.2.7. Virtual Page Implementation

VPage.WaitUntilInCore

live: $\Box\Diamond(\sim DFree.empty) \wedge (\Box\Diamond(\sim MFree.empty) \vee \Diamond\Box(InCore)) \wedge$
$\qquad \Box\Diamond(InCore) \supset$
$\qquad\qquad \Diamond(\text{after } WaitUntilInCore)$

VPage.ThrowOut

live: $\Box\Diamond(\sim DFree.empty) \wedge (\Box\Diamond(\sim MFree.empty) \vee \Diamond\Box(InCore)) \supset$
$\qquad \Diamond(\text{after } ThrowOut) \wedge \Diamond(\sim InCore)$

We also must specify the auxiliary functions:

$$InCore \wedge \Box(\sim \text{after } clear \wedge \sim \text{after } ThrowOut) \supset \Box(InCore)$$

$$\sim InCore \wedge \Box(\sim \text{after } fetch \wedge \sim \text{after } assign) \supset \Box(\sim InCore)$$

$$cleared \supset \sim InCore$$

$$cleared \wedge \Box(\sim \text{after } fetch \wedge \sim \text{after } assign) \supset \Box(cleared)$$

$$\sim cleared \wedge \Box(\sim \text{after } clear) \supset \Box(\sim cleared).$$

The two VPage invariants state that this VirtualPage module has permission to access no more than one MainStore page and one DrumStore page at a time:

$$|Mowns[\text{MyId}]| \leq 1 \quad \wedge \quad (|Mowns[\text{MyId}]| = 1 \equiv InCore) \qquad (1)$$

$$|Downs[\text{MyId}]| \leq 1, \qquad (2)$$

where MyId is the index of the VirtualPage of which this VPage is a part and $|S|$ denotes the number of elements in set S. Assertion (2) implies

$$\Box(\sim DFree.empty),$$

because there are only V copies of the VirtualPage module and each can have permission to access at most one DrumStore page, there must always be free DrumStore pages ($V < D$). This result simplifies the services above by eliminating the $\Box\Diamond(\sim DFree.empty)$ clause from each hypothesis.

The VPage commitment states that when a page is removed from the MainStore, that page must be released to MFree:

$$InCore \wedge \Diamond(\sim InCore) \supset \Diamond(\sim MFree.empty). \qquad (3)$$

Clerk Specification

The clerk is a simple monitor; it is used for communication between the boss and the CyclicDiscarder.

7.2.7.   Virtual Page Implementation

clerk.signal

live: $\Diamond(\textit{after signal}) \wedge \Diamond(\textit{signalled})$

clerk.WaitForSignal

live: $\Box\Diamond(\textit{signalled}) \quad \supset$
$\Diamond(\textit{after WaitForSignal})$

Boss Specification

The *boss* process is best described by its code:

```
loop
        VPage.WaitUntilInCore
        clerk.WaitForSignal
        VPage.ThrowOut
end loop
```

The *boss* is specified by a single commitment:

$$\Diamond(\textit{VPage.InCore}) \wedge \Box\Diamond(\textit{clerk.signalled}) \quad \supset \quad \Diamond(\sim \textit{MFree.empty}).$$

This commitment follows directly from the live-assertions of the procedures it calls and the commitment (3).

▶**Proof of** Boss Commitment:

Assume $\Diamond(\textit{InCore}) \wedge \Box\Diamond(\textit{signalled})$. Since *InCore* becomes true, it will eventually become false or will remain true forever:

$$\Diamond(\textit{InCore} \wedge \Diamond(\sim \textit{InCore})), \quad \text{or} \qquad \text{(case1)}$$

$$\Diamond\Box(\textit{InCore}). \qquad \text{(case2)}$$

In case 1, *VPage* commitment (3) allows us to conclude

$$\Diamond(\sim \textit{MFree.empty}),$$

which is the desired result. In case 2, the hypotheses of the live-assertions for the three statements that constitute the *boss* become permanently satisfied.

7.2.7. Virtual Page Implementation

Therefore, we can infer that

$$\square\diamond(after\ ThrowOut),$$

and hence,

$$\square\diamond(\sim InCore)$$

Commitment (3) then implies

$$\diamond(\sim MFree.empty). \qquad \blacksquare$$

VirtualPage: Specification Matches Implementation

In order to prove that the *VPage* services correctly implement the *Virtual-Page* services, we must show that

$$\forall v\big(\square\diamond(VirtualStore[v].signalled)\big) \quad \supset \quad \square\diamond(\sim MFree.empty). \qquad (4)$$

This will allow us to replace the hypotheses about *MFree* in the *VPage* service specifications with corresponding hypotheses about *signalled*, which the *Cyclic-Discarder* process will guarantee to be true.

If we assume that (for each *clerk*)

$$\square\diamond clerk.signalled,$$

then, each *boss* will guarantee that

$$\diamond(InCore) \supset \diamond(\sim MFree.empty). \qquad (5)$$

We prove (4) by contradiction.

▶**Proof of** (4):

Suppose that the following assertion is true:

$$\forall v\big(\square\diamond(VirtualStore[v].signalled)\big) \quad \wedge \quad \diamond\square(MFree.empty) \qquad (6)$$

By invariant MF1 and assertion (1), we can then deduce that *m* *VirtualPages* control *MainPages*; the *m* *VPages* have *InCore* = *true*. But by assertion (5), each of these *VirtualPages* promises that

$$\diamond(\sim MFree.empty),$$

which contradicts assertion (6). $\quad\blacksquare$

We have shown that the *VirtualPage* services are implemented correctly. The next step in the proof would be to show that the *VPage* specifications are implemented correctly in the code.

7.2.7.   Virtual Page Implementation

VirtualPage Safety

> **Heuristic 11.**   *Make virtual data structures explicit.*

In order to reason about the contents of the virtual page, we shall provide an auxiliary virtual page called *MyPage*, which is an auxiliary array of words. We prove from the code of the *VPage* monitor that every time an operation is executed that modifies the *MainStore* page corresponding to this virtual page, *MyPage* is modified in the same way. Similarly, we show that any changes made to *MyPage* occur only when it corresponds to a *MainStore* page, and that the *MainStore* page is modified in exactly the same way. Therefore, the contents of *MyPage* (if the virtual page is not cleared) is always equal to the contents of one *MainStore* page or one *DrumStore* page. If there is a copy of *MyPage* in both the *MainStore* and the *DrumStore* then the contents of all three are equal.

The proof that the contents of *MyPage* always equals the contents of the implemented pages is an invariant of the implementation of the *VPage* monitor, and therefore requires a proof that involves the internal variables of the monitor. In the following discussion, the variable *where* represents the location of the contents of the virtual page: *in* means that the contents are stored in *MainStore[m]*, *out* means that the contents are stored in *DrumStore[d]*, and *cleared* means that the page is all zeros and is not stored. The variable *unchanged* implies that the page is *in* but that it has not be altered since it was copied from disk, and hence the copy in *DrumStore* is still correct. If an unchanged page is to be tossed out of the *MainStore*, then there is no reason to copy it to disk. The following six invariants formalize the instances when physical copies of *MyPage* exist. (Of course, they must be proved from the monitor's code):

$$where = in \quad \supset \quad m \in Mowns[MyId] \qquad (VPI1)$$
$$where = in \quad \supset \quad MyPage = MainStore[m] \qquad (VPI2)$$
$$where = in \wedge unchanged \quad \supset \quad d \in Downs[MyId] \qquad (VPI3)$$
$$where = in \wedge unchanged \quad \supset \quad MyPage = DrumStore[d] \qquad (VPI4)$$
$$where = out \quad \supset \quad d \in Downs[MyId] \qquad (VPI5)$$
$$where = out \quad \supset \quad MyPage = DrumStore[d] \qquad (VPI6)$$

The statement that there is always one physical copy of a non-clear *MyPage* is the immediate result of

$$where \neq clear \quad \supset \quad where = in \vee where = out,$$

7.2.7. *Virtual Page Implementation*

Having proven that *MyPage* is always "represented" in either the *Drum-Store* or the *MainStore*, we can conclude the discussion of safety begun in Section 7.2.5. Suppose we can prove the following statement about program S' that uses a *MainStore* with V pages,

$$\{P\}S'\{Q\},$$

Transforming S' back to S allows us to use the a similar proof to show

$$\{P\}S\{Q\},$$

because each action of S that accesses the *MainStore* has the same effect as the corresponding action of S' on the enlarged *MainStore*. Between those operations, *MyPage* cannot change, so even if the page is swapped out and then brought back, it will be unchanged.

Chapter 8
Conclusion

This thesis has extended the art of program verification in two directions. First, it has incorporated structured programming (modularization) and temporal logic as tools for proving the correctness of parallel programs, including both safety and liveness properties. Second, it has significantly extended the work of Stenning and others in the field of specifying and verifying network protocols that are written in a high-level language. In addition, this thesis attempted to present some useful heuristics to aid others in constructing such proofs.

In Chapters 2, 3, and 4, we laid the foundation for the new results of this thesis. We first presented an overview of the language constructs that we would use to specify parallel programs. We then reviewed the history of the program verification techniques that contributed directly to the technique developed in this thesis. Finally, we described temporal logic as a notation suitable for expressing liveness properties of programs.

In Chapter 5, we presented the verification technique used in the rest of the thesis. This presentation took the form of logical inference rules and heuristics. Verifying a program is still more an art than a science, for there are no fixed rules for choosing the right invariant or the correct commitment. The heuristics presented in this section should simplify the search for invariants and commitments that describe the properties of parallel programs.

We presented the new results of this thesis in Chapters 6 and 7. In Chapter 6, we proved the safety and liveness properties of four network protocols from the literature. In these examples, the processes communicated over different types of media and were of different levels of complexity. In Chapter 7, we discussed Hoare's structured paging system as an example of a resource allocation problem. The presentation emphasized the ability of invariants, commitments, and service specifications to specify the safety and liveness properties of a complex program. These two chapters served to demonstrate that the techniques presented in this thesis can be applied to problems that approach real-world complexity.

As I mentioned in the introduction, this thesis should apply to both the areas of program verification and program design. If verification is ever going to have a significant impact on the programming community, then it must become part of the job of specifying, designing, and writing a program. Verification serves as a formal means for specifying the problem, for checking to see that intermediate designs correspond to the specifications, and for showing that the final code has not introduced any new logic errors. Verification is not a panacea.

8. Conclusion

It will not eliminate the need for testing, because it does not deal with efficiency or with performance. It does not supplant the need for documentation, because the logic only states what should be done, not how or why it was done. As systems grow larger and as more people become involved in a given project, the need for a standard way to specify interfaces between modules and for a means to determine how well services meet their specifications becomes paramount. Verification helps meet this need.

What is left to be done? Verification is still fighting for acceptability. More tools (such as temporal logic) are needed to make the job of program verification easier. Much research has gone into the field of automatic program verification. An excellent example of that work is the Stanford Pascal verifier [25]. It is an interactive program that aids the programmer in specifying and proving properties of a program. Incorporating the axioms for temporal logic into the verifier poses no obvious problems [26].

In the area of network protocols, there are at least two directions in which this thesis can be extended. First, more complicated link-level protocols can be specified and verified using the parallel-program model; one candidate would be HDLC [4, 5]. Second, other types of protocols can be verified, including connection control [44], file transfer, routing, broadcast [46], and data encryption [8].

There have been few attempts to prove correctness of resource allocation programs [36]. In many cases, new techniques and new notations will be required to simplify the task of describing and verifying complex resource allocation problems. For example, distributed programs in which there is no central representation of the system state are not adequately verified by the current techniques. In such programs, the state may be composed of the states of several submodules, or many versions of the state may exist in different submodules. Both situations are difficult to specify and to verify, because monitor invariants, which represent much of the state information, are valid only when the monitors are free, and it may never be the case that all of the monitors are free at the same time [2]. Another resource allocation problem occurs when resources on different levels of a system can be proved to be live individually, but deadlock can occur when they are combined. For example, disk space allocation can be proved to be free from deadlock and so can allocation of tape drives, but if one user requests disk space first and another user requests tape drives first, there is a potential deadlock [49].

In conclusion, we state one additional heuristic that should cover those situations not otherwise discussed in this thesis.

> **Heuristic 12.** *If the first eleven heuristics do not suffice, call me.*

Appendix A
Temporal Logic (Derived Theorems)

This appendix presents Pnueli's axiom system **DX** for temporal logic and some theorems that have proved useful in this thesis. The first section of the appendix lists axioms, theorems, and inference rules of non-temporal logic used in the proof of the temporal theorems [28]. The next three sections consist of Pnueli's axioms and inference rules. The final section is the *tool-box* of temporal theorems and their contrapositives.

Axioms and Derived Rules of Standard Logic

$\lambda, A \vdash A$ .... Assumption Axiom

$$\frac{\lambda \vdash B}{\lambda, A \vdash B}$$ Assumption Intro

$$\frac{\lambda, A \vdash B \ \ \& \ \ \lambda, \sim A \vdash B}{\lambda \vdash B}$$ Assumption Elim

$\lambda \vdash T$ .... T Axiom

$\lambda \vdash \sim F$ .... F Axiom

$$\frac{\lambda \vdash A}{\lambda \vdash A \vee B}$$ $\vee$ Intro

$$\frac{\lambda, A \vdash C \ \ \& \ \ \lambda, B \vdash C \ \ \& \ \ \lambda \vdash A \vee B}{\lambda \vdash C}$$ $\vee$ Elim

$$\frac{\lambda \vdash A \ \ \& \ \ \lambda \vdash B}{\lambda \vdash A \wedge B}$$ $\wedge$ Intro

$$\frac{\lambda \vdash A \wedge B}{\lambda \vdash A}$$ $\wedge$ Elim

$$\frac{\lambda, A \vdash B}{\lambda \vdash A \supset B}$$ $\supset$ Intro

$$\frac{\lambda \vdash A \ \ \& \ \ \lambda \vdash A \supset B}{\lambda \vdash B}$$ $\supset$ Elim (*Modus ponens*)

$$\frac{\lambda, A \vdash B \ \ \& \ \ \lambda, A \vdash \sim B}{\lambda \vdash \sim A}$$ $\sim$ Intro

$$\frac{\lambda \vdash A \ \ \& \ \ \lambda \vdash \sim A}{\lambda \vdash B}$$ $\sim$ Elim

$$\frac{\lambda \vdash A}{\lambda \vdash \sim \sim A}$$ $\sim \sim$ Intro

$$\frac{\lambda \vdash \sim \sim A}{\lambda \vdash A}$$ $\sim \sim$ Elim

$$\frac{\lambda \vdash A \supset B \ \ \& \ \ \lambda \vdash B \supset A}{\lambda \vdash A \equiv B}$$ $\equiv$ Intro

A. Temporal Logic (Derived Theorems)

$$\frac{\lambda \vdash A \equiv B}{\lambda \vdash A \supset B} \qquad\qquad \equiv \text{ Elim}$$

$(A \supset (B \supset C)) \;\equiv\; ((A \wedge B) \supset C)$ $\supset$ to $\wedge$ Transform

$((A \vee B) \wedge (\sim A)) \;\supset\; B$ $\vee$ Elim'

$((A \supset B) \wedge (\sim B)) \;\supset\; (\sim A)$ $\supset$ Elim' (*Modus Tollens*)

$((A \supset C) \wedge (B \supset C)) \;\equiv\; ((A \vee B) \supset C)$ Proof by cases

$((A \supset B) \wedge (B \supset C)) \;\supset\; (A \supset C)$ $\supset$ Transitivity

$((A \equiv B) \wedge (B \equiv C)) \;\supset\; (A \equiv C)$ $\equiv$ Transitivity

$(A \supset B) \;\equiv\; (\sim A \vee B)$ $\supset$ to $\vee$ Transform

$\sim(A \vee B) \;\equiv\; (\sim A \wedge \sim B)$ DM

$\sim(A \wedge B) \;\equiv\; (\sim A \vee \sim B)$ DM'

$(A \supset B) \;\equiv\; (\sim B \supset \sim A)$ CP

$(A \wedge B) \;\equiv\; (B \wedge A)$ $\wedge$ Commutativity

$(A \vee B) \;\equiv\; (B \vee A)$ $\vee$ Commutativity

$(A \equiv B) \;\equiv\; (B \equiv A)$ $\equiv$ Commutativity

The System DX: Axioms

The **DX** system contains three temporal operators: $\square$, $\lozenge$, and $\circ$. They are interpreted as henceforth, eventually, and next-instant.

$\lozenge P \;\equiv\; \sim\square\sim P$	A0
$\square(P \supset Q) \;\supset\; (\square P \supset \square Q)$	A1
$\square P \;\supset\; P$	A2
$\circ(\sim P) \;\equiv\; \sim(\circ P)$	A3
$\circ(P \supset Q) \;\supset\; (\circ P \supset \circ Q)$	A4
$\square P \;\supset\; \circ P$	A5
$\square P \;\supset\; \circ\square P$	A6
$\square(P \supset \circ P) \;\supset\; (P \supset \square P)$	A7
$\sim\lozenge\sim P \;\equiv\; \square P$	A0'
$(\square P \wedge \lozenge Q) \;\supset\; \lozenge(P \wedge Q)$	A1'
$P \;\supset\; \lozenge P$	A2'
$\circ P \;\supset\; \lozenge P$	A5'
$\circ\lozenge P \;\supset\; \lozenge P$	A6'
$(P \wedge \lozenge(\sim P)) \;\supset\; \lozenge(P \wedge \circ(\sim P))$	A7'
$\square(\circ P \supset P) \;\supset\; (\lozenge P \supset P)$	A7''

A. Temporal Logic (Derived Theorems)

The System DX: Inference Rules

$$\frac{A \text{ is an instance of a Tautology}}{\vdash A} \quad \text{TAU}$$

$$\frac{\vdash A \ \& \ \vdash (A \supset B)}{\vdash B} \quad \text{MP}$$

$$\frac{\vdash A}{\vdash \Box A} \quad \text{GEN}$$

The System DX: Derived Inference Rules

$$\frac{A \vdash B}{\vdash (\Box A \supset B)} \quad \text{DED}$$

$$\frac{\vdash (A \equiv B)}{\vdash (W(A) \equiv W(B))} \quad \text{EQU}$$

$$\Box(\Box P \supset \Box Q) \ \lor \ \Box(\Box Q \supset \Box P) \quad \text{D2 Theorem}$$

$$\Box(\Box(P \supset \Box P) \supset P) \ \supset \ (\Diamond \Box P \supset P) \quad \text{N1 Theorem}$$

The System DX: Theorems

$$\circ - GEN. \quad \frac{\vdash A}{\vdash OA}$$

1. $ASSUME \vdash A$
2. $\vdash \Box A$ GEN
3. $\vdash OA$ A5,MP ■

$Hyp - sub. \quad (((A \land B) \supset C) \land (D \supset B)) \supset ((A \land D) \supset C)$

1. $(((A \land B) \supset C) \land (D \supset B) \land (A \land D)) \supset A$ $\land$ Elim
2. $(((A \land B) \supset C) \land (D \supset B) \land (A \land D)) \supset D$ $\land$ Elim
3. $(((A \land B) \supset C) \land (D \supset B) \land (A \land D)) \supset (D \supset B)$ $\land$ Elim
4. $(((A \land B) \supset C) \land (D \supset B) \land (A \land D)) \supset B$ $\supset$ Elim
5. $(((A \land B) \supset C) \land (D \supset B) \land (A \land D)) \supset A \land B$ $\land$ Intro
6. $(((A \land B) \supset C) \land (D \supset B) \land (A \land D)) \supset ((A \land B) \supset C)$ $\land$ Elim
7. $(((A \land B) \supset C) \land (D \supset B) \land (A \land D)) \supset C$ $\supset$ Elim
8. $(((A \land B) \supset C) \land (D \supset B)) \supset ((A \land D) \supset C)$ $\supset$ to $\land$ Transform ■

A. Temporal Logic (Derived Theorems)

$Hyp-intro.$ $(A \supset B)$ $\supset$ $((A \lor C) \supset (B \lor C))$

1. $(A \supset B) \land A$	$\supset$	B	$\supset$ Elim
2. $(A \supset B) \land A$	$\supset$	$B \lor C$	$\lor$ Intro
3. $(A \supset B) \land C$	$\supset$	C	Assumption Axiom
4. $(A \supset B) \land C$	$\supset$	$B \lor C$	$\lor$ Intro and Commutativity
5. A	$\supset$	$((A \supset B) \supset (B \lor C))$	$\supset$ to $\land$ Transform, $\land$ Commutativity
6. C	$\supset$	$((A \supset B) \supset (B \lor C))$	$\supset$ to $\land$ Transform, $\land$ Commutativity
7. $(A \lor C)$	$\supset$	$((A \supset B) \supset (B \lor C))$	Proof by Cases
8. $((A \lor C) \land (A \supset B))$	$\supset$	$(B \lor C)$	Proof by Cases
9. $(A \supset B)$	$\supset$	$((A \lor C) \supset (B \lor C))$	$\land$ Commutativity, $\supset$ to $\land$ Transform ∎

1. $\Box\Box P \equiv \Box P$

   1. $\Box\Box P \supset \Box P$ A2 $(P \to \Box P)$

   1. $\Box P \supset \circ\Box P$ A6
   2. $\Box(\Box P \supset \circ\Box P)$ GEN
   3. $\Box P \supset \Box\Box P$ A7   ∎

1'. $\Diamond\Diamond P \equiv \Diamond P$

2. $\Box(P \land Q) \equiv (\Box P \land \Box Q)$

   1. $(P \land Q) \supset P$ $\land$ Elim
   2. $\Box((P \land Q) \supset P)$ GEN
   3. $\Box(P \land Q) \supset \Box P$ A1
   4. $\Box(P \land Q) \supset \Box Q$ Symmetry
   5. $\Box(P \land Q) \supset (\Box P \land \Box Q)$ $\land$ Intro

   1. $(P \land Q) \supset (P \land Q)$ Assumption Axiom
   2. $P \supset (Q \supset (P \land Q))$ $\supset$ to $\land$ Transform
   3. $\Box(P \supset (Q \supset (P \land Q)))$ GEN
   4. $\Box P \supset \Box(Q \supset (P \land Q))$ A1
   5. $\Box P \supset (\Box Q \supset \Box(P \land Q))$ A1, EQU
   6. $(\Box P \land \Box Q) \supset \Box(P \land Q)$ $\supset$ to $\land$ Transform   ∎

2'. $\Diamond(P \lor Q) \equiv (\Diamond P \lor \Diamond Q)$

3. $\Diamond(P \supset Q) \equiv (\Box P \supset \Diamond Q)$

   1. $\Diamond(P \supset Q) \equiv \Diamond(\sim P \lor Q)$ $\supset$ to $\lor$ Transform, EQU
   2. $\Diamond(\sim P \lor Q) \equiv \Diamond \sim P \lor \Diamond Q$ THM 2'., EQU
   3. $\Diamond \sim P \lor \Diamond Q \equiv \sim \Box P \lor \Diamond Q$ A0, EQU
   4. $\sim \Box P \lor \Diamond Q \equiv (\Box P \supset \Diamond Q)$ $\supset$ to $\lor$ Transform
   5. $\Diamond(P \supset Q) \equiv (\Box P \supset \Diamond Q)$ $\equiv$ Transitivity   ∎

A. Temporal Logic (Derived Theorems)

4. $\circ(P \wedge Q) \equiv (\circ P \wedge \circ Q)$

    1. $(P \wedge Q) \supset P$ $\wedge$ Elim
    2. $\circ((P \wedge Q) \supset P)$ $\circ$-GEN
    3. $\circ(P \wedge Q) \supset \circ P$ A4
    4. $\circ(P \wedge Q) \supset \circ Q$ Symmetry
    5. $\circ(P \wedge Q) \supset (\circ P \wedge \circ Q)$ $\wedge$ Intro

    1. $\circ(P \supset R) \supset (\circ P \supset \circ R)$ A4
    2. $\circ(\sim P \vee R) \supset (\sim \circ P \vee \circ R)$ $\supset$ to $\vee$ Transform, EQU
    3. $\circ(\sim P \vee R) \supset (\circ \sim P \vee \circ R)$ A3, EQU
    4. $\sim(\circ \sim P \vee \circ R) \supset \sim \circ(\sim P \vee R)$ CP
    5. $(\circ P \wedge \circ \sim R) \supset \circ(P \wedge \sim R)$ DM, A3, $\sim\sim$ ELIM, EQU
    6. $(\circ P \wedge \circ Q) \supset \circ(P \wedge Q)$ $(\sim R \rightarrow Q)$ ■

4′. $\circ(P \vee Q) \equiv (\circ P \vee \circ Q)$

5. $(P \wedge \circ\square P) \equiv \square P$

    1. $\square P \supset P$ A2
    2. $\circ\square P \supset \circ P$ $\circ$-GEN, A4
    3. $\square P \supset \circ\square P$ A6
    4. $\circ\square P \supset \circ\circ\square P$ $\circ$-GEN, A4
    5. $\circ\square P \supset (\circ P \wedge \circ\circ\square P)$ $\wedge$ Intro (2,4)
    6. $(P \wedge \circ\square P) \supset (\circ P \wedge \circ\circ\square P)$ Assumption Intro
    7. $(P \wedge \circ\square P) \supset \circ(P \wedge \circ\square P)$ THM 4., EQU
    8. $\square((P \wedge \circ\square P) \supset \circ(P \wedge \circ\square P))$ GEN
    9. $(P \wedge \circ\square P) \supset \square(P \wedge \circ\square P)$ A7
  10. $(P \wedge \circ\square P) \supset (\square P \wedge \square\circ\square P)$ THM 2., EQU
  11. $(P \wedge \circ\square P) \supset \square P$ $\wedge$ Elim

    1. $\square P \supset P$ A2
    2. $\square P \supset \circ\square P$ A6
    3. $\square P \supset (P \wedge \circ\square P)$ $\wedge$ Intro   ■

5′. $(P \vee \circ\diamond P) \equiv \diamond P$

6. $\square P \supset \square\circ P$

    1. $\square P \supset \circ P$ A5
    2. $\square(\square P \supset \circ P)$ GEN
    3. $\square\square P \supset \square\circ P$ A1
    4. $\square P \supset \square\circ P$ THM 1., EQU   ■

6′. $\diamond\circ P \supset \diamond P$

A. Temporal Logic (Derived Theorems)

7. $(P \wedge \Box \circ P) \equiv \Box P$

1.	$\Box \circ P \supset \circ P$	A2
2.	$\Box \circ P \supset \circ \Box \circ P$	A6
3.	$\Box \circ P \supset (\circ P \wedge \circ \Box \circ P)$	$\wedge$ Intro
4.	$(P \wedge \Box \circ P) \supset (\circ P \wedge \circ \Box \circ P)$	Assumption Intro
5.	$(P \wedge \Box \circ P) \supset \circ(P \wedge \Box \circ P)$	THM 4., EQU
6.	$\Box((P \wedge \Box \circ P) \supset \circ(P \wedge \Box \circ P))$	GEN
7.	$(P \wedge \Box \circ P) \supset \Box(P \wedge \Box \circ P)$	A7
8.	$(P \wedge \Box \circ P) \supset (\Box P \wedge \Box \Box \circ P)$	THM 2., EQU
9.	$(P \wedge \Box \circ P) \supset \Box P$	$\wedge$ Elim

1.	$\Box P \supset P$	A2
2.	$\Box P \supset \Box \circ P$	THM 6.
3.	$\Box P \supset (P \wedge \Box \circ P)$	$\wedge$ Intro ∎

7'. $(P \vee \Diamond \circ P) \equiv \Diamond P$

8. $\circ \Box P \equiv \Box \circ P$

1.	$\Box P \supset \Box \circ P$	THM 6.
2.	$\circ \Box P \supset \circ \Box \circ P$	O-GEN, A4
3.	$\Box P \supset P$	A2
4.	$\circ \Box P \supset \circ P$	O-GEN, A4
5.	$\circ \Box P \supset (\circ P \wedge \circ \Box \circ P)$	$\wedge$ Intro (2,4)
6.	$\circ \Box P \supset \Box \circ P$	THM 5., EQU

1.	$\Box \circ P \supset \circ P$	A2
2.	$\Box \circ P \supset \circ \Box \circ P$	A6
3.	$\Box \circ P \supset (\circ P \wedge \circ \Box \circ P)$	$\wedge$ Intro
4.	$\Box \circ P \supset \circ(P \wedge \Box \circ P)$	THM 4., EQU
5.	$\Box \circ P \supset \circ \Box P$	THM 7., EQU ∎

8'. $\Diamond \circ P \equiv \circ \Diamond P$

9. $\Box(P \supset Q) \supset (\Diamond P \supset \Diamond Q)$

1.	$\Box(P \supset Q) \supset \Box(\sim Q \supset \sim P)$	CP, EQU
2.	$\Box(\sim Q \supset \sim P) \supset (\Box \sim Q \supset \Box \sim P)$	A1
3.	$(\Box \sim Q \supset \Box \sim P) \supset (\sim \Diamond Q \supset \sim \Diamond P)$	A0, EQU
4.	$(\sim \Diamond Q \supset \sim \Diamond P) \supset (\Diamond P \supset \Diamond Q)$	CP
5.	$\Box(P \supset Q) \supset (\Diamond P \supset \Diamond Q)$	$\supset$ Transitivity ∎

A. Temporal Logic (Derived Theorems)

10. $\Box P \supset \Box \Diamond P$

    1. $P \supset \Diamond P$ A2′
    2. $\Box(P \supset \Diamond P)$ GEN
    3. $\Box P \supset \Box \Diamond P$ A1   ■

10′. $\Diamond \Box P \supset \Diamond P$

11. $\Box \Diamond \Box P \supset \Box \Diamond P$

    1. $\Diamond \Box P \supset \Diamond P$ THM 10′.
    2. $\Box(\Diamond \Box P \supset \Diamond P)$ GEN
    3. $\Box \Diamond \Box P \supset \Box \Diamond P$ A1   ■

11′. $\Diamond \Box P \supset \Diamond \Box \Diamond P$

12. $\Diamond \Box P \supset \Box \Diamond P$

    1. $\Box P \supset \Box \Box P$ A6
    2. $\Box(\Box P \supset \Box \Box P)$ GEN
    3. $\Diamond \Box P \supset \Diamond \Box \Box P$ THM 9.
    4. $\Diamond \Box P \supset \Diamond \Diamond \Box P$ THM 8′., EQU
    5. $\Box(\Diamond \Box P \supset \Diamond \Diamond \Box P)$ GEN
    6. $\Diamond \Box P \supset \Box \Diamond \Box P$ A7
    7. $\Diamond \Box P \supset \Box \Diamond P$ THM 11., $\supset$ Transitivity   ■

13. $\Box \Diamond \Box P \equiv \Diamond \Box P$

    1. $\Box \Diamond \Box P \supset \Diamond \Box P$ A2

    1. $\Diamond \Box \Box P \supset \Box \Diamond \Box P$ THM 12. $(P \to \Box P)$
    2. $\Diamond \Box P \supset \Box \Diamond \Box P$ THM 1., EQU   ■

13′. $\Diamond \Box \Diamond P \equiv \Box \Diamond P$

14. $\bigcirc(P \supset Q) \equiv (\bigcirc P \supset \bigcirc Q)$

    1. $\bigcirc(P \supset Q) \equiv \bigcirc(\sim P \vee Q)$ CP, EQU
    2. $\bigcirc(\sim P \vee Q) \equiv (\bigcirc \sim P \vee \bigcirc Q)$ THM 4′.
    3. $(\bigcirc \sim P \vee \bigcirc Q) \equiv (\sim \bigcirc P \vee \bigcirc Q)$ A3, EQU
    4. $(\sim \bigcirc P \vee \bigcirc Q) \equiv (\bigcirc P \supset \bigcirc Q)$ CP
    5. $\bigcirc(P \supset Q) \equiv (\bigcirc P \supset \bigcirc Q)$ $\equiv$ Transitivity   ■

A. Temporal Logic (Derived Theorems)

15. $(\Box P \lor \Box Q) \supset \Box(P \lor Q)$

1.	$\Box P \supset P$	A2
2.	$\Box P \supset (P \lor Q)$	∨ Intro
3.	$\Box(\Box P \supset (P \lor Q))$	GEN
4.	$\Box\Box P \supset \Box(P \lor Q)$	A1
5.	$\Box P \supset \Box(P \lor Q)$	THM 1., EQU
6.	$\Box Q \supset \Box(P \lor Q)$	Symmetry
7.	$(\Box P \lor \Box Q) \supset \Box(P \lor Q)$	Proof by cases ∎

15'. $\Diamond(P \land Q) \supset (\Diamond P \land \Diamond Q)$

16*. $\Box(P \lor Q) \supset (\Box P \lor \Diamond Q)$

1.	$(P \lor Q) \supset (\sim P \supset Q)$	$\supset$ to ∨ Transform
2.	$\Box(P \lor Q) \supset \Box(\sim P \supset Q)$	GEN, A1
3.	$\Box(\sim P \supset Q) \supset (\Diamond \sim P \supset \Diamond Q)$	THM 9.
4.	$\Box(P \lor Q) \supset (\Box P \lor \Diamond Q)$	$\supset$ to ∨ Transform, EQU, A0' ∎

16'. $(\Diamond P \land \Box Q) \supset \Diamond(P \land Q)$

16''. $\Box(P \lor Q) \supset (\Diamond P \lor \Box Q)$

1.		Symmetry on THM 16. ∎

17*. $\Box(P \lor Q) \supset (\Box \Diamond P \lor \Box \Diamond Q)$

1.	$\Box(P \lor Q) \supset (\Box P \lor \Diamond Q)$	THM 16.
2.	$\Box\Box(P \lor Q) \supset \Box(\Box P \lor \Diamond Q)$	GEN, A1
3.	$\Box(\Box P \lor \Diamond Q) \supset (\Diamond\Box P \lor \Box\Diamond Q)$	THM 16''.
4.	$\Box\Box(P \lor Q) \supset (\Diamond\Box P \lor \Box\Diamond Q)$	$\supset$ Transitivity (2,3)
5.	$\Box(P \lor Q) \supset \Box\Box(P \lor Q)$	THM 1.
6.	$\Box(P \lor Q) \supset (\Diamond\Box P \lor \Box\Diamond Q)$	$\supset$ Transitivity (4,5)
7.	$\Diamond\Box P \supset \Box\Diamond P$	THM 12.
8.	$(\Diamond\Box P \lor \Box\Diamond Q) \supset (\Box\Diamond P \lor \Box\Diamond Q)$	Hyp-intro
9.	$\Box(P \lor Q) \supset (\Box\Diamond P \lor \Box\Diamond Q)$	$\supset$ Transitivity (6,8) ∎

17'. $(\Diamond\Box P \land \Diamond\Box Q) \supset \Diamond(P \land Q)$

---

*I would like to thank T. J. Myers for his help with theorems 16 and 17.

A. Temporal Logic (Derived Theorems)

18. $\lozenge\square(P \wedge Q) \equiv (\lozenge\square P \wedge \lozenge\square Q)$

1.	$\lozenge\square(P \wedge Q) \supset \lozenge(\square P \wedge \square Q)$	THM 2., EQU
2.	$\lozenge(\square P \wedge \square Q) \supset (\lozenge\square P \wedge \lozenge\square Q)$	THM 15′.
3.	$\lozenge\square(P \wedge Q) \supset (\lozenge\square P \wedge \lozenge\square Q)$	$\supset$ Transitivity

1.	$\square\lozenge(P \vee Q) \supset \square(\lozenge P \vee \lozenge Q)$	THM 2′., EQU
2.	$\square(\lozenge P \vee \lozenge Q) \supset (\square\lozenge\lozenge P \vee \square\lozenge\lozenge Q)$	THM 17.
3.	$(\square\lozenge\lozenge P \vee \square\lozenge\lozenge Q) \supset (\square\lozenge P \vee \square\lozenge Q)$	THM 1′., EQU
4.	$\square\lozenge(P \vee Q) \supset (\square\lozenge P \vee \square\lozenge Q)$	$\supset$ Transitivity
5.	$(\lozenge\square P \wedge \lozenge\square Q) \supset \lozenge\square(P \wedge Q)$	CP ∎

18′. $\square\lozenge(P \vee Q) \equiv (\square\lozenge P \vee \square\lozenge Q)$

Appendix B

Hoare's Structured Paging System: The Program

```
type
      MainPageFrame = 0 .. M-1
      DrumPageFrame = 0 .. D-1
      VirtualPageFrame = 0 .. V-1
      cell = 0 .. C-1
      word = { one machine word }
      page = array cell of word
var
      MainStore: array MainPageFrame of page
      DrumStore: array DrumPageFrame of page


MFree: monitor
var
      pool: set of ( MainPageFrame )
      owns: private [ VirtualPageFrame ] set of ( MainPageFrame )

visible procedure acquire ( var m: MainPageFrame )
begin
      wait ( ~empty ( pool ) )
      m := AnyOneOf ( pool )
      pool := pool - m
      owns [ id ]  := owns [ id ]  + m
end procedure

visible procedure release ( m: MainPageFrame )
begin
      pool := pool + m
      owns [ id ]  := owns [ id ]  - m
end procedure

auxiliary function empty ≡ empty ( pool )

begin
      InitialiseFull ( pool )
      ∀ i ∈ VirtualPageFrame ( InitialiseEmpty ( owns [ i ] ) )
end monitor { MFree }
```

Global Declarations and MFree Monitor

B. Hoare's Structured Paging System: The Program

```
DFree: monitor
var
     pool: set of (DrumPageFrame)
     owns: private [VirtualPageFrame] set of (DrumPageFrame)

visible procedure acquire(var d: DrumPageFrame)
begin
     wait (~empty(pool))
     d := AnyOneOf(pool)
     pool:= pool - d
     owns [id] := owns [id] + d
end procedure

visible procedure release(d: DrumPageFrame)
begin
     pool := pool + d
     owns [id] := owns [id] - d
end procedure

auxiliary function empty ≡ empty(pool)

begin
     InitialiseFull(pool)
     ∀ i ∈ VirtualPageFrame (InitialiseEmpty(owns [i]))
end monitor {DFree}
```

DFree Monitor

B. Hoare's Structured Paging System: The Program

drum: module = (drummer, DrumHardware; input, output)

drummer: monitor
    var
          direction: (in, out, null)
          m: MainPageFrame
          d: DrumPageFrame
          finished: boolean
          working: private [VirtualPageFrame] of boolean
              { used for proof of drummer }

          DrumStore: array DrumPageFrame of page

    visible procedure input (dest: MainPageFrame; source: DrumPageFrame)
    begin
        wait (direction = null)
        working [id] := true
        direction := in
        m := dest
        d := source
        finished := false
        wait (finished)
        direction := null
        working [id] := false
    end procedure

    visible procedure output (dest: DrumPageFrame; source: MainPageFrame)
    begin
        wait (direction = null)
        working [id] := true
        direction := out
        m := source
        d := dest
        finished := false
        wait (finished)
        direction := null
        working [id] := false
    end procedure

Drum Module: Drummer Monitor (part 1)

B. Hoare's Structured Paging System: The Program

```
    visible procedure execute
    begin
        case direction of
            in:
                    MainStore.CopyDtoM(d,m)
            out:
                    MainStore.CopyMtoD(m,d)
            null:
                    { do nothing for one revolution }
        end case

        finished := true
    end procedure

    auxiliary function idle ≡ direction = null

    auxiliary function finished ≡ finished

begin
    direction := null
    finished := true
    ∀ i ∈ VirtualPageFrame(working[i] := false)
end monitor { drummer }

DrumHardware: process
begin
    loop
            drummer.execute
    end loop
end process { DrumHardware }

moduleprocedure input(dest: MainPageFrame; source: DrumPageFrame)
    ≡ drummer.input(dest, source)

moduleprocedure output(dest: DrumPageFrame; source: MainPageFrame)
    ≡ drummer.output(dest, source)

end module { drum }
```

Drum Module: Drummer Monitor (part 2) and DrumHardware

B. Hoare's Structured Paging System: The Program

```
VirtualMemory: module = ( VirtualStore, CyclicDiscarder;
                          fetch, assign, clear)


VirtualStore: array [ VirtualPageFrame ] of VirtualPage


CyclicDiscarder: process
var
      v: VirtualPageFrame
begin
      loop
            for v ∈ VirtualPageFrame do
                  VirtualStore [ v ] .signal
                  { wait a while }
            od
      end loop
end process { CyclicDiscarder }


moduleprocedure fetch( v: VirtualPageFrame; l: line; var w: word )
      ≡ VirtualStore [ v ] .fetch( l, w )

moduleprocedure assign( v: VirtualPageFrame; l:line; w: word )
      ≡ VirtualStore [ v ] .assign( l, w )

moduleprocedure clear( v: VirtualPageFrame )
      ≡ VirtualStore [ v ] .clear
```

VirtualMemory Module: Cyclic Discarder

B. Hoare's Structured Paging System: The Program

VirtualPage: module template = (*VPage, boss, clerk;*
                        fetch, assign, clear, signal)

VPage: monitor
    var
        where: (*in, out, cleared*)
        m: *MainPageFrame*
        d: *DrumPageFrame*
        unchanged: boolean
        MyPage: auxiliary page

    procedure *BringIn*
    begin
        if *where* ≠ *in* **then**

                MFree.acquire (*m*)
                { *this is the only place where*
                MFree.acquire *is called* }

                if *where* = *cleared* **then**
                      MainStore.clear (*m*)
                      unchanged := *false*
                else { *where* = *out* }
                      drum.input (*m, d*)
                      unchanged := *true*
                fi

                where := *in*
                { *this is the only place where*
                "*where*" *is set to in* }

        fi
    end procedure

VirtualPage Module: VPage Monitor (part 1)

B. Hoare's Structured Paging System: The Program

```
visible procedure WaitUntilInCore
begin
        wait ( where = in )
end procedure



visible procedure ThrowOut
begin
        if where = in then
                if ~unchanged then
                        d := DFree.acquire
                        drum.output ( m, d )
                fi

                where := out
                { this is the only place where
                 "where" is set to out }

                MFree.release ( m )
                { this is the only place where
                 MFree.release is called }
        fi
end procedure



visible procedure fetch ( c: cell; var w: word )
begin
        BringIn
        MainStore.fetch ( m,c,w )  { w := MainStore [ m,c ] }
end procedure
```

VirtualPage Module: VPage Monitor (part 2)

B. Hoare's Structured Paging System: The Program

```
visible procedure assign(c:cell; w:word)
begin
      BringIn
      MainStore.assign(m,c,w) {MainStore[m, c] := w}
      MyPage[c] := w
      if unchanged then
            DFree.release(d)
            unchanged := false
      fi
end procedure


visible procedure clear
begin
      case where of
            in:
                  if unchanged then
                        DFree.release(d)
                  fi
                  MFree.release(m)
            out:
                  DFree.release(d)
            cleared:
                  {do nothing}
      end case
      where := cleared
      ∀ i (MyPage[i] := 0)
end procedure


auxiliary function InCore ≡ where=in

auxiliary function cleared ≡ where=cleared


begin
      where := cleared
end monitor {VPage}
```

VirtualPage Module: VPage Monitor (part 3)

B. Hoare's Structured Paging System: The Program

```
clerk. monitor
     var
           signalled: boolean

     visible procedure signal
     begin
           signalled := true
     end procedure

     visible procedure WaitForSignal
     begin
           signalled := false
           wait ( signalled )
     end procedure

     auxiliary function signalled ≡ signalled
begin
     signalled := false
end monitor { clerk }


boss: process
begin
     loop
           VPage. WaitUntilInCore
           clerk. WaitForSignal
           VPage. ThrowOut
     end loop
end process { boss }

moduleprocedure fetch ( c: cell; var w: word )
     ≡ VPage.fetch ( c, w )
moduleprocedure assign ( c: cell; w:word )
     ≡ VPage.assign ( c, w )
moduleprocedure clear ≡ VPage.clear
moduleprocedure signal ≡ clerk.signal
auxiliary moduleprocedure signalled ≡ clerk.signalled


end module template { VirtualPage }
end module { VirtualMemory }
```

VirtualPage Module: Clerk Monitor and Boss

References

1] K. A. Bartlett, R. A. Scantlebury, and P. T. Wilkinson.
A note on reliable full-duplex transmission over half-duplex links.
Communications of the ACM, 12 (5):260–261, May 1969.

2] A. J. Bernstein and F. B. Schneider.
On restrictions to ensure reproducible behavior in concurrent programs.
TR79-374, Department of Computer Science, Cornell University, March 1979.

3] Gregor V. Bochmann and Jan Gecsei.
A unified method for the specification and verification of protocols.
Proceedings of IFIP Congress 77, pages 229–234. North Holland Publishing Company, 1977.

4] Daniel Brand and William H. Joyner, Jr.
Verification of HDLC.
IBM Research Report 33661, Yorktown Heights, New York, July 1979.

5] J. Bremer and O. Drobnik.
A new approach to protocol design and validation.
IBM Research Report 34789, Yorktown Heights, New York, December 1979.

6] Per Brinch Hansen.
Operating System Principles.
Prentice-Hall, Englewood Cliffs, New Jersey, 1973.

7] Per Brinch Hansen.
Network: A multiprocessor program.
IEEE Transactions on Software Engineering, SE-4 (3):194–199, May 1978.

8] Peter J. Denning, personal communication, April 1980.

9] Robert W. Floyd.
Assigning meanings to programs.
Proceedings of Symposia in Applied Mathematics XIX, pages 19–32, American Mathematical Society, 1967.

References

10] Dov Gabbay, Amir Pnueli, Sharon Shelah, Yonatan Stavi.
On the temporal analysis of fairness.
Seventh Annual ACM Symposium on Principles of Programming Languages (Las Vegas), pages 163–173. ACM, January 1980.

11] Charles M. Geschke, James H. Morris Jr., and Edwin H. Satterthwaite.
Early experience with Mesa.
Communications of the ACM, **20** (8):540–553, August 1977.

12] Donald I. Good and Richard M. Cohen.
Principles of proving concurrent programs in Gypsy.
Sixth Annual ACM Symposium on Principles of Programming Languages (San Antonio), pages 42–52. ACM, January 1979.

13] John V. Guttag, Ellis Horowitz, and David Musser.
Abstract data types and software validation.
Communications of the ACM, **21** (12):1048–1064, December 1978.

14] Paul Hilfinger, Gary Feldman, Robert Fitzgerald, Izumi Kimura, Ralph L. London, KVS Prasad, VR Prasad, Jonathan Rosenberg, Mary Shaw, and William A. Wulf (editor).
An informal definition of Alphard (preliminary).
CMU-CS-78-105, Computer Science Department, Carnegie-Mellon University, February 1978.

15] C. A. R. Hoare.
An axiomatic basis for computer programming.
Communications of the ACM, **12** (10):576+, October 1969.

16] C. A. R. Hoare.
Towards a theory of parallel programming.
In Hoare and Perrott, editors, *Operating Systems Techniques*. Academic Press, 1972.

17] C. A. R. Hoare.
A structured paging system.
Computer Journal, **16** (3):209–215, August 1973.

18] C. A. R. Hoare.
Monitors: An operating system structuring concept.
Communications of the ACM, **17** (10):549–557, October 1974.

References

19] C. A. R. Hoare.
     Communicating sequential processes.
     Communications of the ACM, **21** (8):666–677, August 1978.

20] John H. Howard.
     Proving monitors.
     Communications of the ACM, **19** (5):273–279, May 1976.

21] John H. Howard.
     Signaling in monitors.
     Second International Conference on Software Engineering (San Francisco),
         pages 47–52. IEEE, October 1976.

22] G. E. Hughes and M. J. Cresswell.
     An Introduction to Modal Logic.
     Methuen and Co. Ltd., London, 1968.
     Distributed in the United States by Harper and Row.

23] Leslie Lamport.
     "Sometime" is sometimes "not never": On the temporal logic of programs.
     Seventh Annual ACM Symposium on Principles of Programming Languages (Las Vegas), pages 174–185. ACM, January 1980.

24] Barbara Liskov, Alan Snyder, Russell Atkinson, and Craig Schaffert.
     Abstraction mechanisms in CLU.
     Communications of the ACM, **20** (8):564–576, August 1977.

25] D. C. Luckham, S. M. German, F. W. von Henke, R. A. Karp, P. W.
         Milne, D. C. Oppen, W. Polak, W. L. Scherlis.
     Stanford PASCAL Verifier User Manual.
     STAN-CS-79-731, Computer Science Department, Stanford University,
         April 1979.

26] David C. Luckham, personal communication, May 1980.

27] W. C. Lynch.
     Reliable full-duplex file transmission over half-duplex telephone lines.
     Communications of the ACM, **11** (6):407–410, June 1968.

28] Zohar Manna.
     Mathematical Theory of Computation.
     McGraw-Hill, 1974.

References

29] Zohar Manna and Amir Pnueli.
Axiomatic approach to total correctness of programs.
Acta Informatica, **3** :243–263, 1974.

30] John M. McQuillan and Vinton G. Cerf.
Tutorial: A Practical View of Computer Communications Protocols.
IEEE Computer Society, 1978.

31] James G. Mitchell, William Maybury, and Richard Sweet.
Mesa language manual (version 5.0).
CSL-79-3, Xerox Palo Alto Research Center, April 1979.

32] Susan S. Owicki.
Axiomatic Proof Techniques for Parallel Programs.
PhD thesis, TR75-251, Department of Computer Science, Cornell University, July 1975.

33] Susan S. Owicki and David Gries.
Verifying properties of parallel programs: An axiomatic approach.
Communication of the ACM, **19** (5):279–285, May 1976.

34] Susan S. Owicki.
Specifications and proofs for abstract data types in concurrent programs.
In F. L. Bauer and M. Broy, editors, *Program Construction*, pages 174–197. Springer-Verlag, 1979.

35] Susan S. Owicki.
Specification and verification of a network mail system.
In F. L. Bauer and M. Broy, editors, *Program Construction*, pages 198–234. Springer-Verlag, 1979.

36] Susan S. Owicki.
Verifying parallel programs with resource allocation.
In E. K. Blum, M. Paul, and S. Takasu, editors, *Mathematical Studies of Information Processing*, pages 151–163. Springer-Verlag, 1979.

37] Amir Pnueli.
The temporal logic of programs.
The 18th Annual Symposium on Foundations of Computer Science (Providence, Rhode Island), pages 46–57. IEEE, October 1977.

References

38] Amir Pnueli.
A temporal semantics for concurrent programs.
Unpublished, University of Pennsylvania, November 1977.

39] Amir Pnueli.
The temporal semantics of concurrent programs.
Semantics of Concurrent Computation, pages 1–20. Springer-Verlag, 1979.

40] Nicholas Rescher and Alasdair Urquhart.
Temporal Logic.
Springer-Verlag (Library of Exact Philosophy), 1971.

41] Harry Rudin, Colin H. West, and Pitro Zafiropulo.
Automated protocol validation: One chain of development.
IBM Research Report 29762, Zurich, January 1978.

42] Mary Shaw, William A. Wulf, and Ralph L. London.
Abstraction and verification in Alphard: Defining and specifying iteration
and generators.
Communications of the ACM, 20 (8):553–564, August 1977.

43] Norman V. Stenning.
A data transfer protocol.
Computer Networks, 1 (2):99–110, September 1976.

44] Norman V. Stenning.
Definition and Verification of Computer Network Protocols.
PhD Thesis, University of Sussex, 1978.
NPL Report DNACS 15/79, National Physical Laboratory, U. K., 1979.

45] Carl A. Sunshine.
Formal techniques for protocol specification and verification.
Computer, 12 (9):20–27, September 1979.

46] David W. Wall
Mechanisms for Broadcast and Selective Broadcast
PhD thesis, Computer Science Department, Stanford University.
Technical report 190, Computer Systems Laboratory, Stanford University,
June 1980.

References

47] Colin H. West.
Computer-aided validation of communication protocols.
IBM Research Report 27959, Zurich, March 1977.

48] Colin H. West.
A general technique for communications protocol validation.
IBM Research Report 29095, Zurich, October 1977.

49] Gio Wiederhold, personal communication, July 1980.

Vol. 77: G. V. Bochmann, Architecture of Distributed Computer Systems. VIII, 238 pages. 1979.

Vol. 78: M. Gordon, R. Milner and C. Wadsworth, Edinburgh LCF. VIII, 159 pages. 1979.

Vol. 79: Language Design and Programming Methodology. Proceedings, 1979. Edited by J. Tobias. IX, 255 pages. 1980.

Vol. 80: Pictorial Information Systems. Edited by S. K. Chang and K. S. Fu. IX, 445 pages. 1980.

Vol. 81: Data Base Techniques for Pictorial Applications. Proceedings, 1979. Edited by A. Blaser. XI, 599 pages. 1980.

Vol. 82: J. G. Sanderson, A Relational Theory of Computing. VI, 147 pages. 1980.

Vol. 83: International Symposium Programming. Proceedings, 1980. Edited by B. Robinet. VII, 341 pages. 1980.

Vol. 84: Net Theory and Applications. Proceedings, 1979. Edited by W. Brauer. XIII, 537 Seiten. 1980.

Vol. 85: Automata, Languages and Programming. Proceedings, 1980. Edited by J. de Bakker and J. van Leeuwen. VIII, 671 pages. 1980.

Vol. 86: Abstract Software Specifications. Proceedings, 1979. Edited by D. Bjørner. XIII, 567 pages. 1980

Vol. 87: 5th Conference on Automated Deduction. Proceedings, 1980. Edited by W. Bibel and R. Kowalski. VII, 385 pages. 1980.

Vol. 88: Mathematical Foundations of Computer Science 1980. Proceedings, 1980. Edited by P. Dembiński. VIII, 723 pages. 1980.

Vol. 89: Computer Aided Design - Modelling, Systems Engineering, CAD-Systems. Proceedings, 1980. Edited by J. Encarnacao. XIV, 461 pages. 1980.

Vol. 90: D. M. Sandford, Using Sophisticated Models in Resolution Theorem Proving.
XI, 239 pages. 1980

Vol. 91: D. Wood, Grammar and L Forms: An Introduction. IX, 314 pages. 1980.

Vol. 92: R. Milner, A Calculus of Communication Systems. VI, 171 pages. 1980.

Vol. 93: A. Nijholt, Context-Free Grammars: Covers, Normal Forms, and Parsing. VII, 253 pages. 1980.

Vol. 94: Semantics-Directed Compiler Generation. Proceedings, 1980. Edited by N. D. Jones. V, 489 pages. 1980.

Vol. 95: Ch. D. Marlin, Coroutines. XII, 246 pages. 1980.

Vol. 96: J. L. Peterson, Computer Programs for Spelling Correction: VI, 213 pages. 1980.

Vol. 97: S. Osaki and T. Nishio, Reliability Evaluation of Some Fault-Tolerant Computer Architectures. VI, 129 pages. 1980.

Vol. 98: Towards a Formal Description of Ada. Edited by D. Bjørner and O. N. Oest. XIV, 630 pages. 1980.

Vol. 99: I. Guessarian, Algebraic Semantics. XI, 158 pages. 1981.

Vol. 100: Graphtheoretic Concepts in Computer Science. Edited by H. Noltemeier. X, 403 pages. 1981.

Vol. 101: A. Thayse, Boolean Calculus of Differences. VII, 144 pages. 1981.

Vol. 102: J. H. Davenport, On the Integration of Algebraic Functions. 1–197 pages. 1981.

Vol. 103: H. Ledgard, A. Singer, J. Whiteside, Directions in Human Factors of Interactive Systems. VI, 190 pages. 1981.

Vol. 104: Theoretical Computer Science. Ed. by P. Deussen. VII, 261 pages. 1981.

Vol. 105: B. W. Lampson, M. Paul, H. J. Siegert, Distributed Systems – Architecture and Implementation. XIII, 510 pages. 1981.

Vol. 106: The Programming Language Ada. Reference Manual. X, 243 pages. 1981.

Vol. 107: International Colloquium on Formalization of Programming Concepts. Proceedings. Edited by J. Diaz and I. Ramos. VII, 478 pages. 1981.

Vol. 108: Graph Theory and Algorithms. Edited by N. Saito and T. Nishizeki. VI, 216 pages. 1981.

Vol. 109: Digital Image Processing Systems. Edited by L. Bolc and Zenon Kulpa. V, 353 pages. 1981.

Vol. 110: W. Dehning, H. Essig, S. Maass, The Adaptation of Virtual Man-Computer Interfaces to User Requirements in Dialogs. X, 142 pages. 1981.

Vol. 111: CONPAR 81. Edited by W. Händler. XI, 508 pages. 1981

Vol. 112: CAAP '81. Proceedings. Edited by G. Astesiano and C. Böhm. VI, 364 pages. 1981.

Vol. 113: E.-E. Doberkat, Stochastic Automata: Stability, Nondeterminism, and Prediction. IX, 135 pages. 1981.

Vol. 114: B. Liskov, CLU, Reference Manual. VIII, 190 pages. 1981.

Vol. 115: Automata, Languages and Programming. Edited by S. Even and O. Kariv. VIII, 552 pages. 1981.

Vol. 116: M. A. Casanova, The Concurrency Control Problem for Database Systems. VII, 175 pages. 1981.

Vol. 117: Fundamentals of Computation Theory. Proceedings, 1981. Edited by F. Gécseg. XI, 471 pages. 1981.

Vol. 118: Mathematical Foundations of Computer Science 1981. Proceedings, 1981. Edited by J. Gruska and M. Chytil. XI, 589 pages. 1981.

Vol. 119: G. Hirst, Anaphora in Natural Language Understanding: A Survey. XIII, 128 pages. 1981.

Vol. 120: L. B. Rall, Automatic Differentiation: Techniques and Applications. VIII, 165 pages. 1981.

Vol. 121: Z. Zlatev, J. Wasniewski, and K. Schaumburg, Y12M Solution of Large and Sparse Systems of Linear Algebraic Equations. IX, 128 pages. 1981.

Vol. 122: Algorithms in Modern Mathematics and Computer Science. Proceedings, 1979. Edited by A. P. Ershov and D. E. Knuth. XI, 487 pages. 1981.

Vol. 123: Trends in Information Processing Systems. Proceedings, 1981. Edited by A. J. W. Duijvestijn and P. C. Lockemann. XI, 349 pages. 1981.

Vol. 124: W. Polak, Compiler Specification and Verification. XIII, 269 pages. 1981.

Vol. 125: Logic of Programs. Proceedings, 1979. Edited by E. Engeler. V, 245 pages. 1981.

Vol. 126: Microcomputer System Design. Proceedings, 1981. Edited by M. J. Flynn, N. R. Harris, and D. P. McCarthy. VII, 397 pages. 1982.

Voll. 127: Y. Wallach, Alternating Sequential/Parallel Processing. X, 329 pages. 1982.

Vol. 128: P. Branquart, G. Louis, P. Wodon, An Analytical Description of CHILL, the CCITT High Level Language. VI, 277 pages. 1982.

Vol. 129: B. T. Hailpern, Verifying Concurrent Processes Using Temporal Logic. VIII, 208 pages. 1982.